30-

THIS VOLUME IS THE FIRST OF A SERIES ON THE GRAPHIC ARTS
AND THE ARTS OF THE BOOK, PUBLISHED BY THE AMERICAN
INSTITUTE OF GRAPHIC ARTS, 115 EAST 40 STREET, NEW YORK

Updike: American Printer

AND HIS

MERRYMOUNT PRESS

NOTES ON THE PRESS AND ITS WORK

BY DANIEL BERKELEY UPDIKE

• • •

WITH A GATHERING OF ESSAYS BY

STANLEY MORISON • GREGG ANDERSON

T. M. CLELAND • M. A. DE WOLFE HOWE

GEORGE PARKER WINSHIP • RUDOLPH RUZICKA

DAVID T. POTTINGER • CARL P. ROLLINS

• • •

AND A GALLERY OF

MERRYMOUNT TITLE-PAGES AND TYPES

NEW YORK

The American Institute of Graphic Arts

1947

THE CONTENTS

UPDIKE · AMERICAN PRINTER

AND HIS

MERRYMOUNT PRESS

DANIEL BERKELEY UPDIKE
FROM A STUDY BY RUDOLPH RUZICKA, 1930

NOTES ON THE PRESS
AND ITS WORK

DANIEL BERKELEY UPDIKE

PRINTING became the occupation of my life by pure accident. Books, as literature, have been familiar to me as long
as I can remember, for my mother, a woman of very remarkable intellectual powers who knew thoroughly both English
and French literature, trained my taste in reading; but I knew
nothing about how books were printed or put together. However, an experience that occurred after my father's death in
1878 familiarized me with the outside and inside of many
volumes I should never have known about otherwise. This
was a winter passed as an assistant at the Providence Athenaeum, when the librarian, being invalided, asked me to
relieve him by taking some hours of duty there each day. I
had access also to the interesting but then crowded library of
Brown University; and when in Newport I spent many hours
among the books at the Redwood Library. All this was done
without any particular aim. How the books were made never
interested me; least of all did it occur to me that I should ever
make books myself. But this substratum of familiarity with
books of all sorts, their appearance, titles, contents, stood me
later in good stead. My mother, who was a thorough student,
was impatient at my miscellaneous and ineffective browsings.
"You are not a scholar," she used to say. "You do not love
to learn as I do." Nor did I love to learn. I was unhappy at
school, and as I look back upon it I had reason to be. The
only thing I ever got there was a deepened religious sense,
for the master, an Episcopal clergyman of real "Evangelical"
piety, in the short daily morning talks before lessons began,
made an impression that I have never forgotten. Eagerness
for knowledge about things I wanted to know was not lacking, but most of the knowledge imparted did not concern the

7

things I wanted to know about. One scar inflicted on me has never been effaced — nor forgiven. On the last Friday of each month a torturing hour was devoted to an exercise called "declamation." I was paralyzed by the necessity of speaking in public, not so much because I feared to speak as because I could put nothing into the dreary selected "pieces" I was set to declaim. Such was my dread of these occasions that by the time the fateful Friday arrived I was ill with apprehension. I trace to these oratorical forced marches a life-long inability to address with ease any assemblage large enough to be considered an audience. By inheritance I ought to have had some capacity in this direction, for my father and my grandfather were both effective speakers. The latter constantly spoke on public questions and was for many years a factor to be reckoned with in the General Assembly, and my father was presiding officer of the Rhode Island House of Representatives during the first two years of the Civil War.

The temporary employment at the Providence Athenaeum of which I have spoken became more regular on the death of the librarian, and I held for a few months the place of assistant to the librarian *pro tempore* until the election of a new librarian-in-chief. Then came the question: what next was I to do? Some members of my family proposed a position in a bank, being ignorant or forgetful of the fact that I could not then (or now) readily add a simple column of figures. Having made this "gesture," and having met with a refusal — which may be numbered among the few wise decisions of a long life — they washed their hands of the matter and me. College was impossible in the state of our affairs and although I ostensibly regretted this, my previous experience of education was so little alluring that I privately counted necessity a virtue.

But in the spring of 1880 this lull was broken by a telegram from a cousin in Boston: "A place is open for you with Houghton, Mifflin & Company." I replied that I would take the position, and the next day I left Providence for the city where I have lived ever since. The place I was given was that of errand boy — I was told that everyone began there in that way, and I certainly did. The firm had been driven by a fire from its quarters in Park Street and occupied some dreary temporary offices in Franklin Street, near Hawley. The installation was provisional, and as uncomfortable and inconvenient as provisional installations generally are. The *personnel* of the office was unattractive, the hours were long, the duties new and wearisome. Later a return was made to Park Street. But by summer I was so tired that at the end of a two-weeks' holiday, after much searching of heart, I gave up the place. Four days later a letter arrived. The firm was so pleased with my efforts and saw in me (God knows why!) so much promise that I could return on shorter time. That was enough to arouse an already-uneasy conscience.

The Park Street offices to which I returned were in a pleasant old house formerly belonging to the Quincy family, fronting the Common, with back windows giving on the Granary Burying-ground. Park Street was still residential, and this situation was an improvement over the Franklin Street quarters. At first my work was much the same. After a time, however, my occupations became a bit more congenial. I began to help the advertising manager in small ways, and was deputed to look through the endless newspapers that came to the firm for notices of its books. It does not seem as if this occupation could have any bearing on my future work as a printer, but it did; for my eye became so trained to the kinds of types employed in the press of the country that I was able to tell at sight from what paper an extract had been cut. My next step was to prepare "copy" for advertisements and, after a while, to direct how it was to be set up; and this led to making up material for catalogues and revising those already made, and trying to put into them some uniformity of arrangement and harmony of style. The havoc that I created for the compositors and the expense I caused the firm did not occur to me, for since I had never seen type and did not know how it was set (no one thinking it worth while to instruct me), I treated it as if it were made of india-rubber. What those extra corrections must have cost the establishment I have never cared to contemplate.

My expensive performances in this direction arose chiefly from a love of order. The only event I recall that had any effect upon my typographic efforts was an exhibition of early books and manuscripts held by Quaritch of London at the old Tremont House. I visited this exhibition several times and in my work for the firm tried to imitate in a modern way some of the early printing displayed, and, as I look back upon it, anticipated by some years the essays of people who had a definite objective and really knew what they were about. In those days knowledge now commonplace enough was not available, nor were axioms current on unity of style and "rhythm, balance, and color" — terms which I yet but dimly understand, but evidences of which (I am told by those who know) are often artlessly exhibited in my own work.

I was in the employ of Houghton, Mifflin & Company for twelve years, broken by one short and one long and delightful stay abroad. My interest in typography was even then so slight that I troubled myself little to see fine books when in great centers, or to visit places where good books could be seen. My aim seems to have been *not* to know about printing, but to forget a work that had been so full of drudgery. On my return from my second journey, which lasted a year, and the most interesting parts of which my mother and I passed in Morocco, Spain, and Italy, I began to be treated as a person who had taste in typographical arrangement — a fact which never would have been discovered if after my departure the work I had been accustomed to do had not shown a sudden slump. Instead, however, of making better terms before returning, I went back to Park Street at my inadequate salary and received compliments instead of the dollars I so much needed. But the return was depressing.

And yet the experience of those years — too long drawn out though they were — was not fruitless. I made in Park Street some lasting friends: Mr. Francis Garrison, with whose opinions I wholly disagreed and whose character I as wholeheartedly admired; Miss Susan Francis, assistant editor of the *Atlantic Monthly*, upon whose efforts a succession of often indolent editors depended for the impeccable scholarship of the magazine; Dr. Abner Post, of the *Medical and Surgical Journal*, which was published there; and many other interesting people—Mr. Howells, Miss Sarah Orne Jewett, Mrs. Fields, Mrs. Bell, Mrs. Whitman, and Mr. Aldrich. In my position I naturally met Dr. Holmes, Mr. Lowell, Mr. Longfellow, Mrs. Stowe; and I remember Miss Ellen Emerson conducting her father to a desk whereon lay a visitor's book in which the old man tremulously signed his name. Aldrich, then editor of the *Atlantic Monthly*, had an office next to mine. His talk was a constant firework of witticisms. I remember how he confused the man on the Common who, for a consideration, permitted one to peep through his telescope, by asking him seriously: "Is Venus naked to the visible eye?"

Mr. Houghton and Mr. Mifflin both had a sincere desire for excellence in book-making. Mr. Houghton, the senior partner, was a Vermont man, and his character had in it much of "the strength of the hills," though I did not perceive it then. His taste typographically was of the sixties, and it was a sound taste of its kind. He had travelled abroad and had met printers like-minded with himself—I remember a line in one of his letters: "The people of Holland are industrious and happy," which was received by the stay-at-homes with derisive smiles. To me his manner appeared somewhat hectoring, and perhaps I had, unconsciously, the power of irritating him. But a gruff and sometimes rasping speech concealed a tender heart for those in trouble, especially if they were old associates or former work-people. I have seen tears in his eyes as he parted from some old friend less fortunate in life than himself, who had come to ask aid, and who was never sent empty away. Mr. Mifflin, of a different outlook on the world, was equally earnest in his wish that the firm publish good and well-made books. To both men a new publication was an event, and they could talk of nothing else until the next publication day with its new books arrived. In particular

I remember Mr. Houghton's pride in a new issue of Webster's Dictionary. Everyone who came to Park Street was told of the Dictionary, shown the Dictionary, and — if possible — made to praise the Dictionary. One day Mr. Edwin Whipple arrived. Mr. Houghton showed him the volume, and gently leading the conversation in the direction of further commendation, asked: "Mr. Whipple, when you don't know the meaning of a word, what do you do?" "Well," said Mr. Whipple meditatively, "I generally use another word."

It was a tradition of the establishment that no one — unless for grave cause — was ever dismissed. Accordingly, when persons were not agreeable to those in authority, the tactic of Louis XIV was adopted whereby it was signified to uncongenial courtiers or those who would not "court" that retirement to a distance from Versailles would be appreciated. There in retirement they languished. Something like that happened to me, though for a quite different reason. The work I was beginning to do with efficiency I could do better under Mr. Mifflin's eye at the Riverside Press than in Boston, and so it was thought best that I should be sent to Cambridge. I was sent there, and I, personally, languished to such an extent that after two years of it I decided it was not worth while to languish more. Meanwhile I had, in an inadequate and half-hearted fashion, learned to set type or, more accurately, learned how it was set. And I then also learned how much time and money I had wasted by not knowing this earlier.

In the summer of 1892, while still at the Riverside Press, I was asked by the rector of Grace Church, New York, the Rev. William Huntington, to help him and some colleagues out of a difficulty. The 1892 revision of the Book of Common Prayer had just been completed, and a "standard copy" on vellum and an edition on paper had been handsomely printed by Theodore DeVinne in his chilly but workmanlike style. The idea unfortunately occurred to Dr. Huntington, Dr. Doane, Bishop of Albany, and some others that a re-issue might be made of this Prayer Book from the existing plates, with margins adorned with symbolic decorative borders. With more haste than discretion they launched the scheme before completing the arrangements for it; and a relative of a member of the committee was chosen to make designs "because he could draw," without much consideration as to whether he could draw what was wanted. When I saw the designs submitted, I also saw the committee's dilemma. The offer of a very decent sum was made if I would plan some general scheme of decoration and select a competent designer. I declined. The offer was doubled. I reluctantly accepted it, and chose Bertram Goodhue to make a series of borders based on the *Benedicite omnia opera*, for which I picked out appropriate texts. In these decorations Goodhue's line was very far from DeVinne's typography, and I fancy it was a painful task for the latter to reprint his uninspired but dignified book with the *appliqués* so continuously, unremittingly (and sometimes unwillingly), supplied by Goodhue and myself. I remember that we begged those in authority to be allowed to omit borders on the Gospel for Good Friday; but this could not be. The borders were to go on *every* page—so the committee had promised—and on every page they accordingly went. The best things about the book were the cover and charming end-papers which Goodhue designed for it. Sad to relate, the edition had an immediate and astounding success! We were congratulated, and we blushed. Our shame was taken for modesty and we were congratulated more! While the book is indeed a strange one, it is by no means so strange as the designs originally made for it. These I preserved until lately as *pièces justificatives* for a performance about which Goodhue and I often exchanged "the augur's wink."

The time spent at the Riverside Press had convinced me that I must do something on my own lines, and through a commission to print an *Altar Book*, which my old friend the late Harold Brown of Rhode Island stood ready to finance, the opportunity was offered.* Had I not had this definite work

* This book I describe on a later page. Mr. Brown and I had already co-operated in the production of a book entitled: *On the Dedications of American Churches. An Enquiry into the Naming of Churches in the United States, some Account of English Dedications, and Suggestions for*

to do I should not have had the courage to leave my position there. Although I did not then know it, I was starting at a fortunate moment. The repercussion of Mr. Morris' work at the Kelmscott Press was greatly felt in New England. The printing of forty years ago is, to guote a friend's words, "just old enough to awaken reminiscences." "What days those were," he adds, "when we first began to realize that beauty could become, even in New England, an integral part of life. What names rush to our minds: Bertram Goodhue, Will Bradley, Carl Heintzemann, Copeland & Day, and dozens of other brave companions from the time when to be young was very heaven, and we all were young!" With all these men I was acquainted, but Goodhue was the only one I knew well. The best and most consistent printing of that time was done at the instance of Mr. F. H. Day and his partner Herbert Copeland. What they printed was little to my taste, for there was about their performances a certain conscious pose of the kind that made Lord Minto say at the soulful house-party: "I hate clever people—they're so damned silly." But their books were the best of that period.

When I left the Riverside Press in 1893, Mr. Mifflin, who liked my work and had come to trust my judgment, was considerably disappointed, and did not conceal his impatience with my projects; but later our happy relations were resumed, and I always saw him once or twice a year as long as he lived. On these occasions he always said the same words, meant as a compliment. "You know," he would exclaim, "I can only say that I think your success *Perfectly Remarkable!*" He was probably right. As I look back upon it, the venture must have seemed to my elders and betters a desperately silly enterprise, and they were quite correct in estimating my valor as ignorance. I required capital and had little; comprehension of my own trade, of which I had less; and business experience, of

future Dedications in the American Church. Compiled by Two Laymen of the Diocese of Rhode Island. This was printed under my direction at the Riverside Press in 1891 while I was still employed there. Neither Mr. Brown nor I had much in common with American Protestantism, and his position theologically was Tractarian or, as it would now be called, Anglo-Catholic, as mine has continued to be.

which I had none at all. I had no equipment whatever when I began work on my own account. My innocence was such that I thought I could obtain orders and have other printers undertake the composition and press-work at my direction; and to differentiate myself from wiser colleagues, I announced—for a short time—that I undertook "decorative printing." The result was that though other printers did my work they charged the prices ordinarily charged to a customer and I had to make what profit I could over and above that. Thus my prices were higher than those of other printers, and higher than was warranted by any betterment I could give the work; and when my results appeared an improvement on current typography, the printers whom I employed copied the feeble thing they called my "style" with varying degrees of success. So I was forced to invest, most unwillingly, in a small amount of type and ornaments, and by this tortuous path I arrived where most printers begin! Perhaps the reason that I survived, in spite of mistakes, was that a simple idea had got hold of me—to make work better for its purpose than was commonly thought worth while, and by having one's own establishment, to be free to do so.

The first quarters occupied by the Press consisted of two connecting rooms on the upper floor of a building at the corner of Beacon Street and Tremont Place. These rooms, which were lofty of stud, had been formerly occupied by an architect, who had installed a tasteful wooden mantel-piece and a hearth on which it was possible to light a fire. The narrow windows, lofty ceilings, and hardwood floor made a good background for some pieces of old furniture, which presented a much better effect than the office equipment of that day. The back room, looking out on an angle of the Boston Athenaeum, was occupied by Mr. J. E. Hill, who did much of the designing of ornament which I required, as well as work on his own account.

The first book printed under my supervision was a volume of selections for each day in the year, compiled by Lucy Bradlee Stone, under the title *Vexilla Regis Quotidie*. The

Riverside Press was responsible for the composition and press-work, but the arrangement of the little volume was mine. Originally privately-printed, it became by the printing of a second edition in 1895 the first book bearing my name as publisher. It was set in a "modernized old style" type.

Several other books were printed while the *Altar Book* was being planned and produced, and before any varied stock of type was acquired. Perhaps the best one was *The Hazard Family of Rhode Island,* 1635-1894, a genealogical book by Caroline Robinson, the expense of production of which was borne by her sister, Sarah Rodman Woodward. This book, issued in 1895, was very carefully schemed and was set up by that conscientious and thorough craftsman, the late Carl Heintzemann of Boston. Its decorations were re-drawn from the fine series used by the eighteenth-century London printer Bowyer—ornaments among the best of their kind, and splendidly used in some of his folios. These embellishments, with strips of Caslon "flowers," were combined in a quarto book set in various sizes of Caslon type.

After a stock of type was acquired, the first volume set up by us was *The Governor's Garden,* by George R. R. Rivers, a romance based on the life of Governor Hutchinson and his house at Milton. I was familiar with this place, which belonged to the author's aunt, Miss Rose Russell, and the garden with its arbors and pleached alleys remained much as the Governor had left it. It occurred to me to illustrate the book with a series of fictitious silhouettes representing the characters of the story. The head-pieces, each one different but all made up of combinations of but two Caslon "units," were the clever arrangement of Mr. John Bianchi, then foreman of our composing-room. What I remember chiefly, however, is the small amount of type I had with which to print, and the patience of the author under the consequent delay. The "period business" is perhaps a bit overdone for the reader's comfort, but its format attracted considerable attention when the book came out in 1896.

The same year saw the second of my few publishing ventures, in Hans Andersen's *The Nightingale*, cleverly illustrated by Mary Newill of the then-popular Birmingham Guild of Handicraft, for whose short-lived magazine *The Quest* we also were agents. My old friend the late Edward Hort New of Oxford contributed some charming illustrations to that periodical, as did Gere, Gaskin, Miss Newill, and others. And in the same year the *Altar Book* appeared.

It was largely the dissatisfaction felt with the "decorated" Prayer Book that suggested the publication of this volume, and Mr. Brown, who was of my way of thinking in such matters, stood ready to back the undertaking. His stipulations were that the book should be as fine a piece of work as I could make it, and that while strictly conforming to the text of those parts of the Book of Common Prayer containing the altar services, it should yet fall in line with missals of an older period. When musical notation is introduced, the canon law of the Episcopal Church allows a departure from the uniformity required for all service books without music. Accordingly a few notes of plain-song were placed before the collect for the First Sunday in Advent, with which the book opened. Thus the book was strictly canonical, and having received the authorization of the Rev. Samuel Hart, the registrar of the Book of Common Prayer, we were able to place "By Authority" on the title-page. Dr. Huntington, when he saw the volume (which he did not much like), exclaimed: " 'By Authority'! We must look into that!" But as when he looked he found nothing to see, we heard no more about it.

To enumerate the difficulties met with at that period in obtaining what is now easily available would take longer to tell than is here desirable. It is enough to say that after various essays a type was designed for the book by Bertram Goodhue, who also drew the borders and initials—no two of the latter exactly alike—the illustrations being by Anning Bell. The amount of work the undertaking involved was increased by the difficulty in obtaining hand-made paper, in cutting the type, and by various troublesome details. And when the type was designed and cast a separate workshop had to be found where it and a hand-press could be installed and a proof-reader could work. For this purpose an office at the corner of Aldine Street and Estes Place, near the South Station, was rented, and there, through a hot summer, the work was carried on. The press-work was placed with DeVinne, who turned out a magnificent piece of work, although he was frankly out of sympathy with the style of the volume. Begun in 1893, the book was finished at Easter, 1896.

Whatever satisfaction I might have taken in its completion was destroyed by my mother's sudden illness and death, which seemed to deprive me of any incentive to continue along the path on which I had set out. Probably I should not have gone on if I had not already had the nucleus of a tiny organization. When at the Riverside Press I had made the acquaintance of Mr. Anselmo Bianchi, and when I started for myself I asked him to join me. This he could not do, since he was bound by an indenture for a certain period of service there, but he suggested his brother as a man suitable for the place. It thus came to pass that John Bianchi came to the Press. He was later joined by his brother Anselmo, who remained with us for several years, finally returning to the Riverside Press in a position which he has developed into an important one. Miss Ellen Powers, also a former employee of Houghton, Mifflin & Company, was acting as proof-reader and accountant at that time. To the loyalty, patience, and confidence of these three, and to friends who supplied work to do, the Press owes its existence in those early and difficult years. In looking back one realizes the truth of Emerson's phrase: "Every man's task is his life preserver."

The following summer I passed abroad. In London I visited Kelmscott House, where I was kindly received by Mr. Cockerell. This was shortly after Mr. Morris' death, and the London Society of Arts and Crafts was at the moment holding an exhibition where the Kelmscott books were magnificently displayed. I remember making some rather ineffective researches at the British Museum, and there meeting Mr. Alfred Pollard; our first contact with the Caslon house was also made at this time. Between this date and 1914 I made several other foreign journeys, but as I travelled chiefly in Spain and places somewhat remote from printing interests these have little to do with this narrative. I did, however, go to Parma on one of these journeys and saw the splendid collection of Bodoni's books preserved in the library there, and I also went to Mainz and Leipzig. And on my last foreign journey I visited the Plantin Museum at Antwerp, partly because I was so tired of saying "No" when anyone asked if I had seen it. I doubt if visits to homes of great and good printing amount to much except from the sentimental point of view. To my mind, a printer can learn more from a few visits to such an exhibition of printed books as is shown in the King's Library of the British Museum than by desultory wanderings to less well arranged and more distant collections.

Owing to the demolition of the Beacon Street building in 1896, the Press, so called, had to go elsewhere, and rooms were secured in a building round the corner, at 7 Tremont Place, in a house formerly, I believe, occupied by the Winthrop family. The ground floor was used by our landlords, Messrs. Ginn & Company, as a shop or shops, and we occupied the next floor, or "noble storey," consisting of two drawing-rooms connected by folding doors and a small side room occupied as a private office. The front room on Tremont Place covered the width of the house, and here a composing-room was installed; the back room, which commanded pleasant glimpses of the Granary Burying-ground, was the general office.

It was while occupying these quarters that I first met Mr. Bruce Rogers. I was already familiar with a book in which he had had a hand—*Notes on the Walters Collection*—so he needed no introduction. The splendid results of his eighteen years' work at the Riverside Press are known of all men. At that early period we saw much of each other, both in town and in country, for in summer I had a country house at Harvard, Massachusetts, where he, Cleland, and others were often visitors.

THE further story of the Press, from this time on, is chiefly the history of such outstanding books as it has printed year by year, save for those years — and they were not uncommon — when nothing interesting is to be chronicled. A connection with the house of T. Y. Crowell & Co. of New York that lasted for a long period was inaugurated in 1897 by the appearance of a book, set in Clarendon type, called *What is Worth While?*, which in my absence abroad was planned by Mr. John Bianchi. This book showed the influence of Mr. Morris' ideas upon commercial work, and the long series of similar 16mo volumes printed for this house followed the general style of the first one, though with varying degrees of success. The covers — rather tasteless affairs — were usually supplied by the publishers, though this first book and *Ships and Havens* had the advantage of a binding designed by Bertram Goodhue.

Our first use of Scotch-face type was made in the same year for Messrs. Crowell & Co. in a little book by Richard Le Gallienne entitled *If I Were God*.

We remained at 7 Tremont Place only two years, for in 1898 another move became necessary when the whole row of old houses had to make way for an office building. The next situation for the Press was 104 Chestnut Street — commonly called (since those were the days of stables in that neighborhood) "Horse Chestnut Street." This house was three stories high, and had two large and two small rooms to a floor. The composing-room was placed on the first floor, the main office on the second at the back, my own office on the same floor at the front, and a proof-readers' room in a hall bedroom. The third story I at first occupied as an apartment.

Later on, in 1903, we utilized the third story as a proof-readers' room and added No. 102 Chestnut Street to No. 104, connecting the lower floors of both houses and using them as a composing-room. The two upper floors of No. 102 I moved into, this apartment being completely separated from the Press.

In 1899 appeared under my imprint a book that had a family

interest, namely, a diary kept by my great-great-uncle, James MacSparran, D.D., between the years 1743 and 1751. MacSparran was an Anglican missionary sent to Rhode Island from London by the Venerable Society for the Propagation of the Gospel in Foreign Parts. There he became rector of St. Paul's Church, Narragansett. His diary is a quaint affair recording the daily life of an American Parson Woodforde. In printing it I conformed to his manuscript — superior letters, odd spelling, and all. This volume was edited by the Rev. Daniel Goodwin, a former rector of the same church.

The Press has been fortunate in its friends, but never more so than in the friendship of Mrs. Wharton. I had known her before she wrote *The Greater Inclination*, her first book of short stories, and when the volume came to be published, in 1899, she stipulated with the Scribners, who issued it, that I should be employed to print it. In this and in all her later books that we printed, we employed a Scotch-face type that, common enough in England then and in America now, had not before been used for fiction in this country. To Mrs. Wharton's thoughtful act the Press owed not merely the prestige of printing her books, but also the printing of many other volumes for Scribner's — indeed we were constantly employed by the firm until it set up a press of its own. Nothing could have helped the Press more, just then, than the Scribner connection, for it showed we were not amateurs but could hold our own with larger printing-houses; and this was all due to the friend who used her influence as generously, intelligently, and effectively then, as many times before and since, for persons or causes that she thought deserved a "lift." Besides the volume mentioned the following books written by Mrs. Wharton were printed here: *The Touchstone* (1900); *Crucial Instances* (1901); *The Valley of Decision* (1902); *Sanctuary* (1903); *Madame de Treymes* (1907).

The most ambitious book of 1900 was printed for Mrs. J. V. L. Pruyn — a description of a pastoral staff given by her to the Diocese of Albany. The pictures of the staff were reproduced in photogravure, which made an odd alliance with a text set throughout in black-letter type. Goodhue designed the elaborate frameworks of the opening pages and, in fact, all the decorations and the binding. The book is an exhibition of his cleverness as a draughtsman rather than of any skill of mine.

In the same year a little book that had a great success was printed for Scribner's, set in Scotch-face type. This was Stevenson's *Christmas Sermon*, bound in boards, with a green cloth back and paper sides of that gloomy shade of blue known to my childhood in Seidlitz powders. This was reprinted several times, and was followed by a number of short essays in the same format. A genealogical book of importance typographically, set throughout in Caslon, was *Mumford Memoirs*, by my old friend the late Dr. James Gregory Mumford. Another genealogy was printed for the late Josiah Henry Benton, the first of a series of books brought out by him. The best of these volumes were the catalogue, set in Mountjoye and Oxford types, of his splendid collection of English and American Prayer Books now in the Boston Public Library; and a memoir of Baskerville, read by Mr. Benton before the Society of Printers and printed later in amplified form—a book now rare and much sought after. For the latter we used a Caslon type of the period when Caslon's fonts showed the influence of Baskerville, and its title-page is a good bit of "period" printing. Between Mr. Benton's wife and my mother's family there was an ancient friendship, though I became aware of this only after our first meeting. Mr. Benton, under a brusque manner, concealed great sensitiveness and a warm heart; but these were not always apparent. On my first visit to him at his office in the Ames Building accompanied by Mr. Bianchi, Benton, expecting to see one person and seeing two, exclaimed: "Who's that? — plumber's helper?"

Possibly the most ambitious "period" book in the so-called colonial style that we ever attempted was an edition in quarto of Irving's *Knickerbocker's History of New York*, printed for R. H. Russell in 1900. The arrangement of its complicated and voluminous preliminary matter I am proud of, and the book "hangs together" in spite of Maxfield Parrish's eight illustrations (then the vogue), which are only pseudo-"colonial." This volume was set up at the Press, though it was printed outside it. A catalogue of Doubleday, Page & Co.'s books also deserves attention for its use of Clarendon type—one of the few times I have used it to my own satisfaction.

Mr. Charles Goodspeed first became a customer in 1901 by commissioning me to print Sanborn's *Personality of Thoreau*. For this slim volume, printed in a limited edition, Scotch-face type, much leaded, was used, printed on a highly calendered paper, with some copies on Japan paper. The result was a somewhat attenuated elegance, but it found favor and was followed by more books in the same style. A more sympathetic piece of work was a little volume printed for Miss Sarah Cooper Hewitt called *Some Old Letters & Bits of History*, a paper written by her aunt, Margaret Adelia Cooper. Its cover of Empire paper, with white label, yellow edges, and endpapers printed from wood-blocks in green and pink, and the Bewickian decorations accord with its leisurely well-bred text. The book-marker in blue and pink was much consulted about, and Miss Hewitt—very much *la maîtresse-femme*—adjured me that under no possible pretence should like endpapers and ribbons adorn the books of any other living being! Only two hundred copies were printed, to be used as gifts.

Two French *bâtarde* types that I acquired in Paris were first used in a tiny rubricated volume printed for Edwin S. Gorham of New York, *The Form of Solemnization of Matrimony*, issued in 1901. We later used the same type in a circular, *Merrymount: Being a few Words on the Derivation of the Name of The Merrymount Press*, brought out after our removal to Summer Street. Of these two interesting fonts, the larger is a true *bâtarde*, the smaller a *lettre de somme*. The same year brought to the Press the service for the consecration of a life-long friend, the late Charles Brent, as Bishop of the Philippines; several of Brent's books we afterwards printed. This service was one of a long series of similar services for consecrations of bishops and of churches, the institution of rectors, and the like, that have been printed here. As these ceremonies usually included a celebration of the Eucharist, we began the composition by first printing the two pages containing the prayer of consecration facing each other and worked back from that point, so there should be no noise of turning leaves at the most solemn moment of the service. All "turn-overs" were planned as far as possible to occur at liturgical points when they would not disturb the congregation: for three thousand people turning a leaf at once gives the effect of the sudden flight of a flock of pigeons.

The year 1902 was marked by my publication of *Four Addresses*, by Henry Lee Higginson. Its cover, as were those of several other books printed at the Press, was designed by Mrs. Henry Whitman, a figure in the artistic circles of Boston, who for many years designed the best of the covers for Houghton, Mifflin & Company's books. She was a woman of taste and charm, though the personal impression she produced was perhaps greater than any definite accomplishment. Somewhat fantastic in phrase and manner, she dealt with us, to use her own words, "very handsomely." I remember at the first exhibition of the Society of Arts and Crafts, in 1897, on seeing a folio leaf of our Latin Tacitus set in Goodhue's Merrymount type, she cried: "Phoebus, what a page!" This year saw also the beginning of a set of octavo books finished in 1903 — *The Life and Works of Charles Lamb* — printed in Scotch-face type and issued in twelve volumes for the Pafraets Book Company of Troy, New York.

The Poet Gray as a Naturalist, edited by Charles Eliot Norton, is an essay based on a copy of a book in Mr. Norton's library — the *Systema Naturae* of Linnaeus — interleaved for annotation and illustration by Thomas Gray. From the textpages and those interleaved a few of the most interesting drawings were chosen for reproduction, and selections from Gray's manuscript notes were also printed. These facsimiles are extraordinary pieces of reproduction. The book was published by Goodspeed in an edition of five hundred copies in November, 1903 — or so the colophon says — though as I recall it, it was early in December and much too late for the Christmas trade. As I look back I am impressed with the casual manner in which I then regarded practical affairs.

Mr. Norton was from the beginning of our work most sympathetic and helpful. We were brought together more particularly because of some projects for an endowed University Press at Cambridge. He gave my own Press one or two books to print, presented it with proofs of interesting types and ornaments, and placed at our disposal any books in his library at Shady Hill. He was a great aid in these early years, before other people had found me out or—what was more important—I had "found" myself. But about the business end of the Press he was always a bit nervous, fearing that it might be diverted from the Service of Beauty to the Worship of Mammon; and he grieved at my "defection," as he considered it, when we abandoned the amateur atmosphere of Chestnut Street for the commercial air of Summer. In vain I pointed out that the presses would go through the floor if we had to install them in Chestnut Street. I had, he thought, gone over to the "enemy," though what particular enemy he was loath to specify. For as work increased it was obvious that however much we enlarged the Chestnut Street quarters we could not go on without printing-presses, since without our own machines our press-work was uneven and expensive. The construction of the Chestnut Street houses would not bear much weight, and if a press-room were built out over the small back-yard, this would consume capital and obstruct light. Wandering about in the neighborhood of the South Station one Sunday afternoon, I found a building just completed on Summer Street, and the top floor, although only a well-built loft, seemed to have possibilities. After much cogitation this floor was taken. Some old glass Directoire doors* I had found

* Of these doors there must have been thirty or more. I purchased three, and Miss Amy Lowell, whom I told about them, bought, characteristically, *all* the rest. Two, possibly four, she placed in her house at Brookline; a few more she gave to her architect, who used them in one or two houses on the water side of Beacon Street, where they can still be seen. The rest Miss Lowell stored in her garage with some idea of ultimately making an *"orangerie"* of them. But this did not come to pass, for through a fire the garage, the doors, and the project went up in smoke together.

in East Cambridge, which formerly figured in the Tremont Street façade of the old Boston Museum, were fitted into "compo board" partitions, arranged as nearly as possible on an axis in a building in which nothing was symmetrical. To the old furniture we had, more pieces were added — notably some fine chairs, the gift of two well-disposed friends; and a collection of framed engravings pertinent to printing was begun. All this gave the rooms a certain effect. Three presses were installed and a decent composing-room was arranged. The offices consisted of an ante-room, a reception room, a counting-room, and a library. It was from this locale that we issued the first of a series of illustrated pamphlets describing the Press. All our work was done here for twenty-eight years. It is amusing to remember with how much perturbation of spirit we made each move, only to regret that it was not made long before.

No particularly interesting book was produced in 1903 except the two-volume set of the poems of Dante Gabriel Rossetti — the Cheyne Walk edition — edited by Herbert Copeland, of Copeland & Day, and with a decorative design on the title-page by T. M. Cleland, who also designed the cover. Set in Caslon throughout, the book somewhat reflects the aesthetic movement of which Rossetti was patron saint. Cleland had been living in Boston a little before this time and occupied a small studio, or office, in Cornhill, which was then more of an old-world locality than now, the picturesque effect of its low brick buildings on the curve of the street being then unspoilt by modern erections. Besides designing, Cleland produced several little books at what he called the Cornhill Press, which, like my own, was a press only because we chose to call it so. Our friendship — and I may add my admiration of his talents and his work — dates from those remote days. He was an idealist — quite impractical — often in difficulties; but he produced delightful things then, as in maturity he has continued to do. Perhaps none of us at that period were very sensible or businesslike, and if we had been would never have been heard of more.

Of the long series of music-books turned out for Messrs. Oliver Ditson Company under the title *The Musicians Library*, the major part consisted of lithographic music, all we contributed being the title-pages and introductory matter. In this connection sheet-music covers should be mentioned. These were executed chiefly for Schirmer of Boston and New York, the larger number being printed for the New York house. For these titles little money was available, and most of them had to be produced in a hurry. How to vary them attractively without expense was the problem. Some could be printed solely from type and type-ornaments, but for those requiring decoration we reproduced designs from the engraved ornamentation of the seventeenth and eighteenth centuries. A collection of such engraved work belonged to the Press, and we drew from these plates and procured others for the purpose. Many of the most successful designs were reproduced from the elaborate and often beautiful *cartouches* on old maps. Others were taken from the *Chinoiseries* of Pillement, designs by the Du Cerceau and other *maîtres ornementistes*, Pompeian wall-paintings, German silhouettes — everything conceivable was pressed into service. We continued to turn out this work until 1914.

Music programs also were brought to the Press to be printed. Among the earliest friends of my undertaking was the late Montgomery Sears, whose house during his lifetime and since has been known for the *musicales* at which famous artists have assisted. The programs for these concerts Mr. Sears always brought personally to the Press to be printed, and these leaflets brought that class of our work into notice, leading to more commissions from other quarters. As I look back on the small beginnings of my establishment, I am grateful for the sympathetic interest in its work that my friends have all along shown. I like to record here in addition to those mentioned in connection with the books I am describing the names of others — and these are by no means all — who in ways great and small have been as friendly as Mr. Sears was in those early days: Bishop Brent; Mrs. John Carter Brown;

Mrs. Harold Brown; Mr. and Mrs. John Nicholas Brown, Sr.; Mr. John Nicholas Brown, Jr.; Mrs. William Gammell; Mr. John Chipman Gray; Miss Eleanor Burges Green; Miss Belle da Costa Greene; Mr. Rowland Hazard; Miss Caroline Hazard; Mrs. Cadwalader Jones; Mrs. William Vail Kellen; Mr. Henry W. Kent; Miss Amy Lowell; Mr. John Pierpont Morgan, Sr.; Mr. John Pierpont Morgan, Jr.; Dr. Charles L. Nichols; Miss Elizabeth Norton; Mrs. J. M. Sears; Mr. Edward Perry War-ren; Professor Barrett Wendell; Mrs. Henry Whitman.

The year 1904 was to us notable for the launching of a type designed for the press by Herbert Horne of London, whose essays in typography in *The Hobby Horse* had already attracted attention. The type was a roman letter of fourteen-point size modelled on early Florentine fonts, named Mont-allegro as an Italian equivalent of "Merrymount." Horne stip-ulated that the first volume printed in it should be designed by him, and for the text he employed his own translation of Ascanio Condivi's life of Michael Angelo, or, as Horne pre-ferred to call him, Michelagnolo Buonarroti. He chose as a format for the book a small square quarto resembling early Florentine wood-cut books, with type closely and solidly set; and he also designed the title-page and initials. This type was afterwards employed in volumes of *The Humanists' Library*, where it had a more open and, I think, more agreeable treat-ment. Horne afterwards designed for other firms two similar types, the Florence and the Riccardi, all three being cut by E. P. Prince, who executed the types used by Morris and Cobden-Sanderson. I have never considered Montallegro a complete success—there is about it a rigidity which makes one con-scious of the type instead of the text. The same year Bertram Goodhue's Merrymount type, hitherto used only in the Altar Book, was utilized for a large folio edition of the *Opera Minora* of Tacitus, a text suggested by Mr. Norton and edited by the late Professor Morris Morgan of Harvard University. Only one hundred copies were printed of this volume, which was designed to display the Merrymount type—a fount solely adapted to an enormous page. I sent specimen pages of the book abroad, and our choice of this text suggested its use to the Doves Press, whose first book, the *Agricola*, appeared in 1901.

Another book which attracted attention for its type was Thackeray's *Letters to an American Family*, printed for the Century Company, New York. Here we employed a Mountjoye (or, as it would now be called, "Bell") font, and although this was not its first use by us, it was our first use of it in a book of popular appeal. This Mountjoye type was much the same, if not the same, as some fonts existing at the Riverside Press known in my time as "copper-face," but afterwards called "Brimmer" because they were first used in an address by Martin Brimmer, delivered at Wellesley College at the opening of the Farnsworth Art School. This address was published in October, 1891, and its format and typography were designed by Mrs. Henry Whitman, who was a great friend of Mr. Brimmer's. Mrs. Whitman also arranged the more ambitious volume by Mr. Brimmer, entitled *Egypt*, which was printed in the same type and published at the Riverside Press in December, 1891.

For the Mountjoye type I traced the history of the font until I found what British type-foundry owned the matrices and then obtained strikes of them for our own casting. As I write, this font (discovered by Mr. Stanley Morison to be the production of John Bell of London, 1745-1831) has just been placed on the market—twenty-nine years after its first use by the Press in a little volume of sketches by Frances Dabney entitled *Saudades*, privately printed in 1903 for Miss Amy Lowell. This same type was also used in 1904 for the text of a fourteen-volume set of the Bible printed in several editions on various papers for the R. H. Hinkley Company of Boston. With the commonplace illustrations we had nothing to do—except to deplore their use; and of the various bindings only those in cloth were ours.

One more book must be mentioned under 1904: *The Letters of Three Dutiful & Affectionate Rhode Island Children to their Honoured Parents*—the children being Master Nicholas,

Miss Hope, and Miss Joanna Brown, whose letters were written between 1779 and 1781. This and two succeeding volumes, *The Course of True Love in Colonial Times*, issued in the next year, and *James Browne—His Writings In Prose and Verse*, printed in 1917, seem to me as good "colonial" typography as the Press has ever put out. But few persons have ever seen these books, for the limited numbers printed were chiefly for family distribution.

A volume devoted to the dedication of the John Carter Brown Library in 1903, issued in 1905, was the beginning of a long connection that still continues with this library, of which I am a member of the board of management. In the following year use was made of the Mountjoye type in *The Life of Benvenuto Cellini*, for Brentano's, New York. The title-page of this edition was designed by Cleland. The edition was a great success, but the early issues are the only ones in which the press-work was executed here. Later editions showed an unfortunate declension in this feature.

In the next year the first volume in *The Humanists' Library* was published. This series was under the general editorship of Lewis Einstein, and Maurice Baring translated for its initial issue Leonardo da Vinci's *Thoughts on Art and Life*. These books employed, as I have said, Horne's Montallegro type, and for them Horne designed the initials and title-pages of the first series, which consisted of four volumes in editions of 303 copies. The other three volumes of the first series were *Erasmus Against War*, edited by J. W. Mackail, brought out in 1907; *Petrarch and the Ancient World*, by Pierre de Nolhac, issued in 1907; and Sidney's *Defence of Poesie*, edited by George Edward Woodberry, issued in 1908.

In January, 1906, we printed a handbook of an exhibition, *The Development of Printing as an Art*, arranged in honor of the bicentenary of Benjamin Franklin by the Society of Printers of Boston. This modest organization—of which I was at one time president—still exists, largely because, having no definite program, it has done such necessary work as occasion has presented. Their show was held at the Boston

Public Library, and I had a hand in the preparation of the text of its catalogue as well as charge of its typography. Many of the specimens exhibited came from our library. A somewhat elaborate volume was also issued in 1906 for the Club of Odd Volumes, Harold Murdock's *Historie of the Life and Death of Sir William Kirkaldy of Grange, Knight*. The decorations and initials for this edition of 114 copies were cut on wood, and although great pains were taken with the entire production, I have never thought the book as successful as it should have been. It was printed from a late Caslon font.

I must mention Mrs. John Lowell Gardner as another good friend to the Press. The pamphlet guide for visitors to her house, Fenway Court, we printed for many years. On each revision I spent a morning there, and Mrs. Gardner and I, acting as "visitors," made a tour of the house, guide-book in hand. In this way we were able to test the convenience of arrangement in each succeeding issue. These mornings were always enlivened by Mrs. Gardner's talk about her acquisitions and the way in which she came to possess them. One of our dealings was, however, less fortunate. Mrs. Gardner had endeavored to have prepared for her a catalogue of her books, and, failing to find the desired co-operation in several quarters, she decided to compile it herself, entitling it *A Choice of Books from the Library of Isabella Stewart Gardner, Fenway Court*. Now the compilation of catalogues, like the keeping of hotels, appears within the powers of most Yankees until they try it; and Mrs. Gardner's cataloguing was no better or worse than the work of most amateurs. When the manuscript was in type I detected so many errors that I was sure there were more, and so I told her. But she was positive that all was right, and in spite of my begging that some competent person might revise the work, she held to her opinion. We accordingly printed the catalogue as it stood, but omitted the imprint of the Press. When the volume was distributed — it was privately-printed in 1906 — numberless errors were found, and the omission of the imprint was (I hoped) thereby accounted for. No one was very happy about the matter, least of all Mrs. Gardner, who corrected in pencil such errors as she caught and sent the book out, its blunders naturally being attributed to our carelessness. Some of my friends (who perhaps did not know Mrs. Gardner) said I should not have "permitted" her to make such mistakes. Mr. Norton in particular was severely critical and declared one evening at Shady Hill, in the presence of a number of people, that I should have insisted that some competent person look over the final proofs. "But I did suggest a very competent person," said I, "and it was not well received." "Whom did you suggest?" asked Mr. Norton. "You, sir," I replied. Everybody laughed, and the point was not labored — nor I belabored further. For some time after this my friendship with Mrs. Gardner, as Horace Walpole said of his with Lady Lucan, "rather waned than improved." But before long the difficulty was forgotten — indeed, we printed in 1922 a companion volume, *A Choice of Manuscripts and Bookbindings from the Library of Isabella Stewart Gardner, Fenway Court*. Mrs. Gardner was then ill and the consultations about the book were held in her motor, in which, rain or shine, she punctually kept any appointment she had made. "You must hurry, hurry," she said one day with a humorous expression. "I am dying, and if we don't make haste I shall die first." She had an indomitable spirit — never more finely shown than in those last years.

The chief work of 1907 was the issue, in three volumes, of a second edition of Wilkins Updike's *History of the Episcopal Church in Narragansett, Rhode Island*. This book, by my grandfather, first published in 1847 in a very casual manner, I had long intended to re-issue, and had collected a mass of material to that end. But when I had assembled it I had neither the time nor the ability to arrange it, and the project lay dormant. As luck would have it, a later rector of this ancient cure, the Rev. Daniel Goodwin (editor of the *MacSparran Diary* already mentioned), was greatly interested in the church's history and was free to edit the work, using the material gathered by me; and no man was better fitted for the work or could have done it better. The book is much more than a history of a country parish. It is the history of the whole countryside, and gives especially a picture of social life and manners in eighteenth-century southern Rhode Island that has been the basis of everything written on the subject from that day to this. Fortunately, too, a distant kinsman of mine, Mr. Moses Goddard of Providence, also much attached to Rhode Island traditions, stood ready to help me out, his only stipulation being that the editor should annotate the work to his heart's content. When the manuscript was complete the amount of text had been enormously increased—fourteen hundred printed pages as against four hundred in the first edition! Encouraged by Dr. McVickar, then Bishop of Rhode Island, I cast about for means of publishing the manuscript, which was effected by the aid of several Rhode Island friends: Mr. George Gordon King; Mr. William H. Potter; Mr. George Peabody Wetmore; Mr. William Watts Sherman; and Mr. Goddard, who took the largest share in the production of a book which, alas, he did not live to see completed. A feature of the work is its fifty illustrations, chiefly from portraits hitherto unpublished.

On the publication of the original work in 1847 its author received an honorary degree from Brown University, and the completion of the second edition was signalized by degrees given by Brown University to Dr. Goodwin and to me. The German ambassador Bernstorff received a degree on the same day, and I was deputed by our host at a luncheon afterwards to look after him, since he was not familiar with the intricacies of Providence streets. As we walked along he said to me: "You know, I have to give an address before the alumni of the University this afternoon. I have given twenty such addresses in thirty days. None of them amounted to anything. If I say anything worth hearing I am called to account by Berlin. So my speeches give no pleasure to me nor to anyone else."

The connection of this Press with Brown University began in 1905. The printing of its catalogues set a style somewhat new in college publications—a style widely copied all over this country. Ever since, a large part of the University's "aca-

demic" printing has been done here, and also books such
as Bronson's *History of Brown University* and ephemera for
special occasions, such as the Sesquicentennial of the college,
requiring programs, tickets, orders of service, and the like.

I am often asked if it is not uninteresting to undertake the
printing of catalogues and similar material. As a matter of
fact, such work is often both interesting and difficult, for
in no class of printing is it so necessary to preserve clearness
and simplicity. Refractory tabulation has to be so managed
as to conceal its refractoriness; type arrangements that will
be suitable to all the varying classes of instruction have to be
schemed; and that a college catalogue is a book of reference
has to be kept clearly in view. To the printer such work
appears interesting, to the layman dull. For at the risk of
digression I may add that the attitudes of mind of a professional and of an amateur about printing—as in most forms of
creative endeavor — are quite different. The onlooker sup-
poses the printer to enjoy doing what he enjoys seeing and to
be bored by what bores him; and he also believes that the feeling of a man who does a piece of work successfully is "joy,"
when it is mostly relief. The *problem* is what interests all but
beginners in typography. Its solution may be, and often is,
moderately exciting; although if the problem is successfully
solved no one perceives it has existed. Because all persons who
work realize this, it is easier for one worker to talk to another,
however dissimilar their occupations may be, than it is to
talk with (or to be talked to by) an admirer of one's own
class of work—whose likes or dislikes are often based on
quite the wrong reasons.

A great mass of work for schools, colleges, and institutions
followed in the wake of the academic work for Brown University. Even more important than the printing for Brown has
been a long connection with the Carnegie Foundation for the
Advancement of Teaching. This printing requires ingenuity
in its arrangement and in the co-ordination of material, and
accuracy as absolute as can be attained. The Foundation has
shown the Press much consideration; the Press in turn has

given the best it has. Begun in 1909, the work continues to-day, and will, it is hoped, *ad multos annos.*

A volume of Oakes Ames' *Orchidaceae* — one of a series the Press has since turned out — which showed what could be done typographically with a learned botanical work, and the *Catalogue of a Memorial Exhibition of the Works of Augustus Saint-Gaudens*, printed for the Metropolitan Museum of New York, were the two pieces of work most notable in 1908. The inscriptions in the Saint-Gaudens catalogue presented a problem that was interesting to solve.

An important work printed in six volumes in 1911, at the expense of the late Mr. J. Pierpont Morgan, was the *Archives of the General Convention*, devoted to the correspondence of John Henry Hobart. It was intended to issue more volumes, but the Hobart correspondence was so interminably strung out by the editor and the prospect of arriving at the end of the series became so remote that the project was given up. These severely plain volumes were set in Mountjoye type combined with those Oxford fonts which accord well with it. Another book set in Mountjoye type that was thought successful is the "period" volume, *Letters of Bulwer-Lytton to Macready*, printed for the Carteret Book Club of Newark.

The second series of *The Humanists' Library*, set like the first series in Horne's Montallegro type, was begun in 1912. These volumes we thought great improvements over those of Series I in two respects: (1) by the adoption of a more ample paper-page, and (2) by a reduction of price. The first idea was a good one, the second was not; for collectors, a skittish race unaccustomed to good books at low prices, were thereby scared off, fighting shy of the very feature intended to attract them! And the general public was not interested in such books at all. Both series of *The Humanists' Library* have, however, long been out of print, and so the project justified itself financially. The four volumes in the second series were: *The Correspondence of Philip Sidney and Hubert Languet*, Albrecht Dürer's *Records of Journeys to Venice and the Low Countries*, Pico Della Mirandola's *Platonick Discourse upon Love*, and Della Cassa's *Galateo of Manners & Behaviours*, edited, respectively, by W. A. Bradley, Roger Fry, Edmund G. Gardner, and J. E. Spingarn. Of the title-pages, two were by Cleland and two by W. A. Dwiggins, and plain initials were substituted for the decorated series by Horne used in the first four volumes.

As will be seen, the number of types used by the Press shows little variety. For most books, Caslon, Scotch-face, or the Mountjoye-Oxford combination of fonts is the best, and a departure is desirable only when a new type performs the task to be done better than these types can. But new material — borders, initial-letters, and type-ornaments with which to vary the effect of the types used — was all along acquired, some of it during my several journeys abroad. And here, in parenthesis, I may say that one's attitude towards new movements in typography, and to new types produced under their influence, may be summed up in a comment on literary criticism,* which I adapt to printing: "The new should be welcome, the old not forgotten. What one misses in most contemporary work is a sense of proportion. Men do not remember what has been produced in the past, and do not distinguish between the briefly novel and the permanently valid" — between which one cannot too carefully differentiate. When one sees some ancient type-horror revived as new, one remembers the words of Marie Antoinette's milliner: "There is nothing new except what is forgotten."

The Club of Odd Volumes began to commission the Press to do work as early as 1904. Good examples of the printing for this organization are *A Catalogue of an Exhibition of Waltoniana* (May, 1912) and the more important volume by the late Dr. Charles Lemuel Nichols of Worcester, *Isaiah Thomas, Printer, Writer & Collector*. Both pieces of work were set in Oxford type, and *Isaiah Thomas* is as satisfactory a book in that font as we have ever printed. The most important books of 1913 were the *Ordinary and Canon of the Mass*, printed in Goodhue's Merrymount type, set in double column and

* Sir John Squire.

rubricated; and Mr. F. B. Crowninshield's *Story of George Crowninshield's Yacht, Cleopatra's Barge,* in quarto, set in Scotch-face type, somewhat in the style of the period. The amusing "ship" end-papers were designed by Mr. Dwiggins.

In 1915 Mr. John Bianchi was made a partner as some recognition of effective work in carrying out the aims of the Press and his steadiness and patience in tiding over times of my indifferent health and discouragement at the slow pace of advance. Addressing himself to the problem from a different angle than mine, and bringing to the undertaking thorough knowledge of the processes of production and sound financial judgment, he has always been at one with me in objective. Furthermore, his taste in typography and an instinctive Italian sense of order and proportion have made his collaboration, when planning work or producing it, invaluable.

The *Jonny-Cake Papers of "Shepherd Tom"* ("Shepherd Tom" being Thomas Robinson Hazard) was, like the edition of the *Narragansett Church,* a reprint of a Rhode Island book. It is chiefly notable for its illustrations from pen-and-ink sketches by my old friend Rudolph Ruzicka. It was issued in 1915 and was followed in the next year by another book illustrated by Ruzicka commemorating the fiftieth anniversary of the opening of Vassar College—views of the college buildings enhanced by the introduction of color. But Ruzicka's best-known work for the Press is the series of Annual Keepsakes he has designed and engraved since 1912.

The *Catalogue of the Collection of Prints from the Liber Studiorum of Joseph Mallord William Turner, formed by the late Francis Bullard . . . and bequeathed by him to the Museum of Fine Arts* was printed as a memorial to Mr. Bullard for Mr. Grenville Winthrop, in an edition of three hundred copies for private distribution. It was brought out in 1916. The reproduction of the prints was attended with difficulty, for the originals could not be taken from the Museum, and so trial proofs of each of our plates had to be brought there, compared, and corrected. I have spoken of problems in printing which, if surmounted, should be invisible. There was such a problem in this book. Many of the pictures were not uniform in depth, so that if they were to occupy the same relative position from the top margin of the book throughout, the distance between them and the first line of type, which also had to be invariable in position, differed. We overcame this difficulty by never allowing two pictures to face each other, so that in turning the page the eye did not catch the discrepancy.

The War brought a number of books to the Press in the shape of memorials to single individuals or to groups of men. The most ambitious of these publications is *The Book of the Homeless*, edited by Edith Wharton. Besides the articles in prose and verse contributed by "eminent hands," the illustrations were to be reproductions from a number of original paintings and drawings. To unify all this material was a considerable undertaking, and, when unified, to select the various *media* which would do justice to the originals was a further task. Accordingly, while the title-page and half-titles were printed from blocks engraved by Ruzicka, the illustrations were reproduced by photogravure and in colored half-tone. The latter were printed here. Besides the regular edition, a special issue of 175 copies was printed in a large format with some extra features. The book was sold for the benefit of the American hostels for refugees, and other war charities.

Apropos of Ruzicka's work, in 1917 we printed for the Carteret Book Club of Newark a book illustrated entirely by him. The volume, which was entitled *Newark*, was by Mr. Walter Pritchard Eaton, and the text illustrations were printed at the Press, but the five delightful full-page colored plates Ruzicka printed himself. Another volume brought out in the same year was Percival Merritt's monograph *The Parochial Library of the Eighteenth Century in Christ Church, Boston*, printed to accord with the subject, which made a pretty little "eighteenth-century" volume. Also in 1917 we printed for Brentano's the two-volume edition of Madame Campan's *Memoirs* (in a sense a companion set to the *Cellini* made for the same house), a handsome book set in Mountjoye type. The title-page is a reproduction of an old French engraved title-page; and the cover reproduces a binding said to have been executed by Derôme for Marie Antoinette, called *De Présent*, its design covering uninterruptedly the whole back, the old-fashioned "ribs" being done away with. The bindings of many books printed at the Press have been arranged here. Some of them are simple affairs with cloth backs and marbled cloth or paper sides; others adaptations of old designs which, while not always remarkable, have the advantage of being "on good terms" with the printing inside the cover — which is saying a good deal.

In 1919 we finished the *List of Books Privately Printed by William K. Bixby and those Privately Printed by Book Clubs from Manuscripts in his Collection*. This recalls Mr. Bixby's various brochures printed at this Press, such as *Two Letters of Charles Lamb* and *Martha Washington's Letter*, issued in 1922, which both include facsimiles of the letters themselves. The cover of the Washington letter is an adaptation by Ruzicka of the design of a *toile de Jouy* — an Indian introducing Liberty to the French Monarchy; and this same design was used, though with a different combination of colours, on a reproduction of letters from Wayne and Washington (1922). The most interesting of these books, of which there were a good many, is *Benjamin Franklin on Balloons*. I had chosen for the title-page a reproduction of an old engraving of Franklin's house at Passy, with a Montgolfier balloon riding the sky, and as luck would have it I received at just the right moment a visit from the representative of the French paper-makers Canson and Montgolfier. Finding that the Montgolfier of this firm was a descendant of the famous aeronaut, I procured from him the paper for the booklet, water-marked with a balloon — for the Montgolfier balloon was made of paper from this same mill. For the cover paper an amusing "balloon" design used by Oberkampff for a printed chintz was chosen, being re-drawn for our purpose by Mr. Dwiggins. A quotation on the title-page from Franklin's prophetic letter about the future of air warfare is not the least interesting feature of the book.

In the same year (1919) we printed Part I of the first volume of the Catalogue of the John Carter Brown Library's magnificent collection of Americana—a series still in process. The typographic requirements of this work in diacritical marks, symbols, superior letters, and the like, and the careful proof-reading needful for entries in Latin, Italian, German, Dutch, and other languages make the production one requiring constant care. Three volumes have so far been published, the first two in two parts each, and the third in one.

A Grolier Club edition of Washington Irving's *Notes and Journal of Travel in Europe*, 1804-1805, is specially to be remarked for Ruzicka's three illustrations and title-pages, executed in aquatint with details heightened in water-color. This was issued in three volumes in 1921.

The Wedding Journey of Charles and Martha Babcock Amory was a journal kept by Mrs. Amory during her travels in France, Italy, Switzerland, Holland, and Germany in 1833 and 1834 and afterwards copied by her into a finely-bound blank-book, the tooling of which was reproduced on the binding of the printed volumes. To set up this book seemed an easy task, but as Mrs. Amory's "fine Italian hand" looked legible and wasn't, and as the journey was taken by carriage, the proper names of the less-known towns and villages through which the carriage passed — or sometimes broke down—had to be verified by road-maps of the period. The titles of pictures, statues, and the like, had to be verified from guide-books of that period, for modern guide-books described galleries wholly re-arranged since 1830. The preparation of the manuscript, therefore, proved an almost endless piece of work, and was a triumph of patience and ingenuity. The *résumé* of the contents of chapters, as well as the preface, I wrote myself. The book was issued in two small quarto volumes, and but one hundred copies were printed.

Mrs. Gordon Dexter, for whom the book was printed—great-granddaughter of Copley, grand-niece of Lord Lyndhurst, and daughter of the diarist — was one of the most remarkable figures of the society of her period, and had the most original and distinguished personality I have ever known. Whimsical, unreasoning, autocratic, she belonged to the eighteenth century, and might in appearance have stepped out of one of the many Copley portraits that hung on the walls of her splendid house. Underneath an extremely sophisticated exterior she had the simplicity of a child, and went straight to the heart of matters much as a child does, and sometimes with the same devastating results. She retained her charm to the day of her death. Through all the vicissitudes of life, one trait never varied—Mrs. Dexter's devotion to her mother. These volumes were one of many testimonies to that devotion.

The production, in 1922, of my own book, *Printing Types*, which was printed here though published by the Harvard University Press, came about through an invitation to give some lectures (or, as I preferred to call them, "talks") on printing in the School of Business Administration at Harvard University. As I have said, I have always been tongue-tied when obliged to address an audience, and it was with something akin to panic that I found myself in Cambridge, one late autumn afternoon, to open the course. The subject assigned me was "type and composition," and to veil my inability to speak fluently *ex tempore* I wrote out what I had to expound in as colloquial a style as I could manage, so that I might run for shelter to the manuscript when too confused to remember what I wanted to say next. To my surprise, my efforts appeared to those in authority a success; the lectures were extended to some sixteen sessions, and continued up to the entrance of this country into the War. It was then proposed that these discourses should be made into a book, but since a successful spoken style is by no means satisfactory as a written style, my elaborate informalities had to be transmuted into a more chastened text before they could be printed. This was a terrible job, and would never have been completed except for the help of one of our own force, William Smallfield.* He it

* William H. Smallfield, Jr., was born at Renfrew, Ontario, in 1893, and died at Guelph, Ontario, in 1928. He was of English descent, and of the third generation of a printing family. His grandfather, Albert Smallfield, originally in the employ of the old London firm of Waterlow & Company,

was who hunted up references, verified dates, corrected my grammar, and did the thousand and one odd jobs inherent in the preparation of a work full of names, dates, titles, and like matter requiring accurate transcription. In those last days the "sunny solidity of the *pax Victoriana*" was coming to an end. The lengthening shadows of war darkened too many lives to make the shape of a letter or the characteristics of a font of type seem of importance, and indeed much of the task was in such "hours of gloom fulfilled" that I doubted whether there need be any book at all.

When the text was in final shape, Mr. Bianchi suggested that it would be far more interesting if illustrated. I had not much faith that what I had written would interest anyone, so I saw the value of his suggestion with dismay; for this new plan involved more delay and difficulty. Some of the illustrations I could easily lay my hand on in the library of the Press, but there were many gaps to be filled from books outside it. The Harvard College library, largely through the kindness and influence of the late Archibald Coolidge, let me take rare books from the Library and photograph the required pages; and the Boston Athenaeum and the Pierpont Morgan Library in New York also gave me valuable special privileges. But the Boston Public Library was bound by law to keep certain books in its possession. To meet this requirement a small Irish boy was deputed to represent the Library. Wherever I went he had to go. Thus we passed intermi-

became on his removal to Canada the founder of the *Mercury* of Renfrew, Ontario; and his son, William Smallfield, a man of ability, conducted the paper for nearly fifty years, until its sale in 1919. After a breakdown caused by overwork in assisting his father, the son took a place with us, first as pressman, afterwards as compositor, and, later, when we began to realize his scholarship, as proof-reader and secretary. Sensitive and retiring, a born student, a great reader with a sound taste in literature, he was invaluable to me in the completion of the *Wedding Journey* for Mrs. Gordon Dexter and of my own *Printing Types*. He left us because he thought family duties called him home, but with the hope that he might again take up the position that was always open for him. It was not to be, and after a year or two of invalidism and frustration he died. I like to place beside Smallfield's name the names of two other men sometime of our force: Frank Callan and Walter Vincent Smith. To those who know their histories, these names call up memories of faithfulness, generosity, and fortitude under circumstances in which tragedy had its part. *Lux perpetua luceat eis.*

nable hours that summer in the hot, stifling lofts of photo-engravers, the boy dangling his legs from a bench while I examined negatives of the illustrations. Day after day, I and my unwilling twin left the Library in the morning with books, and wearily returned with them at night. Finally, after infinite labor, the illustrations, the little boy, and I were all "done" together, and the book was printed. By that time I was so convinced that no one would ever read it that I left for a month in the country without seeing the finished volumes. The book has, by those who know, been called a monumental work, and came, so far as I was concerned, fatally near being so. For it I received the medal of the American Institute of Graphic Arts. The issue of three successive editions was no doubt instrumental in bringing me in later years a master's degree from Harvard University and membership in the Massachusetts Historical Society, as well as in the Harvard chapter of the Phi Beta Kappa Society; of this society I am also an honorary member at Brown University. Later on, a paper which originally had been a part of the course of lectures but which was not included in *Printing Types* was combined with two others and issued under the title *In the Day's Work* by the Harvard University Press.

The year 1922 also saw the production of *The Felicities of Sixty*, by I. K. Lionberger, printed for the Club of Odd Volumes in an edition of one hundred copies. For this book we used a font of Dutch type somewhat on the lines of the Fell type, cut by Janson in the seventeenth century, which has long been in our possession. This type we have employed in many of our subsequent books.

Another journal written by a member of the Amory family was produced in the next year, in printing which, as in the former book, expense was not spared. This was *The Journal of Mrs. John Amory*, 1775-1777, issued in an edition of one hundred copies. It was illustrated with some delightful portraits and other material, and was susceptible of interesting treatment typographically. The arrangement of the first page of text is satisfactory, but the title-page would have been improved by making the panel of ornament smaller — reversing the arrangement shown on page one. The cover reproduces a very fine English binding. That same year Mrs. Meyer's *Chinese Painting as Reflected in the Thought and Art of Li Lung-Mien*, 1070-1106, appeared. This volume gave the establishment a reputation for scholarly printing not wholly deserved, for the insertion of lines of Chinese characters had an impressive effect — if one did not know each one was supplied in written form for reproduction by photography and had to be carefully marked "This side up" before we dared place it in the text!

That eccentric English amateur of printing, Edward Rowe Mores, wrote a paper entitled "Of English Founders and Founderies." This was published after his death in 1777, in a very small edition, by John Nichols, who gave it the title by which it has since been commonly known: *A Dissertation upon English Typographical Founders and Founderies*. The book is very queer — its author was even queerer — but it contains a mass of curious information on the subject. I had always been interested in this work, and, after some correspondence, induced the Grolier Club of New York to publish it. The issue of the volume depended, however, on finding someone to write a short introduction. This I offered to do, as our library contained some material for it. The result was that the short introduction became a long one, and the most careful literary performance I have ever attempted, though I have never met more than one or two persons who have taken the trouble to read it. The format of the book was determined by that of Mores' original essay. The decorations, made up from varying combinations of two or three typographical flowers, are worth looking at.

Two books issued in 1925 — more interesting to print or to look at than to read — fell into the category of printing problems. The first was *The Record of Those who Gave to an Endowment Fund collected by The National Society of Colonial Dames of America for the Maintenance of Sulgrave Manor, the Home of the Ancestors of George Washington* — a title

which sufficiently describes what the book is about, and also
suggests that it is scarcely more exciting to the reader than a
telephone directory. Our problem was to make "something"
out of it, and the result was a great folio volume of considerable typographical splendor enhanced by a beautiful heraldic
design by Ruzicka. Forty-eight copies were all that were
needed to supply one copy for Sulgrave Manor and copies for
branches of the Society of Colonial Dames throughout the
country, which subscribed at ten dollars each; and even then
there were a few to spare. A college library purchased the last
example of this unreadable and unread volume for a sum that
would supply a very decent representation of the "world's
best books."

The second volume, printed for the Boston Latin School
Association also in 1925 and entitled *The Public Latin School
of Boston in the World War*, 1914-1918, *A Roll of Honor*,
shows the part played in the war by masters and students of
this ancient school. The book at first sight seems easy to print,
but the proviso that it was to be kept in a glass case and a page
turned every day involved the presentation of entries which
must be complete on each two facing pages. The pages dedi-
cated to men who died in war were rubricated and each
inscription had a page to itself; but for men still living the inscription had — in printer's language — to be "run in." Further
stipulations were (1) that the names should be arranged in
strictly alphabetical order, and (2) that there could be no
omissions in each record. To see how these difficulties were
overcome and the rules complied with, one must see the book.
It was set entirely in Poliphilus and Blado types. The pages
were surrounded by emblematic borders, in which the arms
of the United States, eagles bearing olive branches, and heads
of Liberty, figure in white on black backgrounds — one of the
earliest "native" American type-ornaments, produced just
after the War of 1812. I have had quite enough of books "with
borders on every page," but bordered pages were adopted
here since no more than two pages were to be shown at once.

The Lutetia type designed by J. Van Krimpen we first used

in 1927, in a little book entitled *The Higher Citizenship*, by Alfred L. Baker, and we also employed it for some specimen pages for a folio Book of Common Prayer that were discarded in favor of pages set in Janson type. We also prepared for the Enschedé Foundry of Haarlem, which brought out the Lutetia series, some Latin pages that displayed some of the sizes of this type. In the same year appeared the only book printed at this Press ever placed under a ban: Adam H. Dickey's *Memoirs of Mary Baker Eddy*, set in Mountjoye. The Christian Science authorities suppressed this volume, and as many copies were recalled as possible. To those outside the fold it appears innocuous — and a "collector's item."

The completion of thirty-five years of the work of the Press was signified by an exhibition of Merrymount books in New York under the auspices of the American Institute of Graphic Arts, one book being selected from the output of each year from 1894 to 1928. I was not present at the opening, on the principle that one would rather have it asked why one was not, than why one was, there. But I sent this letter to the president of the Institute, Mr. Frederic Melcher:

"When you kindly suggested an exhibition of the work of the Merrymount Press to inaugurate the use of your new room at the Art Centre, I was only too glad to fall in with the plan; though when it was pointed out that 1928 rounded out thirty-five years in the life of the Press, it caused some searchings of heart. Furthermore, the proposal that the exhibition should be a chronological display of its books presented some very disconcerting possibilities, and reminded me of the proverb that "Old sins have long shadows." In looking back over what (I now realize) is more than a third of a century, instead of having a sense of orderly progression in one's work, these years appear to have been nothing more than (as the late Barrett Wendell said of life) "a confused getting ready to begin." So perhaps my feelings about this thirty-fifth birthday are best expressed by a phrase often used by a great-grandfather of mine, an unworldly man, who kept silk-worms that produced no silk, and wrote a poem called "The Sabbath" that none but his family ever read. When children came to see him on their birthdays, he had, when told their age, an invariable saying which serves me very well now. And this saying was: "What! So old and no better?"

THREE books of typographical interest: *Notes By Lady Louisa Stuart on "George Selwyn and His Contemporaries,"* by John Heneage Jesse, an edition of Walton's *Angler,* and *The Form of Consecration of St. George's Chapel* appeared in 1928. In the Stuart book, printed for the Oxford University Press, New York, a complicated problem was presented, for the original passages in Jesse's *Selwyn* had first to be given, then Lady Louisa's notes upon them, and finally the editor's notes on her annotations. Only a printer can realize the difficulties of getting all these notes on one page — successfully — and yet making a readable volume. The *Angler,* in a small 16mo format, is chiefly remarkable for the delightful *en-têtes* by Mr. Dwiggins, printed in color, and for its cover, also designed by him. The typography was kept simple that it might be subordinate to the illustrative decoration. The St. George's Chapel service is a piece of liturgical printing set in one of Janson's seventeenth-century fonts. Except for rubrication (which is always decorative), it has no ornamentation at all. The cover we designed. Apart from its use, the book had a great success as a piece of typography, and copies have since sold at an absurdly high price.

For the Harvard University Press we printed in 1930 a selection of David Garrick's letters, somewhat whimsically entitled *Pineapples of Finest Flavour.* This also was set in Janson type, and preserves with fidelity the spelling, abbreviations, and peculiarities of the original. It also contains some successful facsimiles of letters. The same year produced an edition of La Fontaine's *Fables,* illustrated with designs engraved on copper by Ruzicka, whose delicate line required a cool and restrained employ of the Janson fonts used. Another book of this period was Caspar Whitney's life of his father-in-law, Charles Adelbert Canfield, in quarto, the first book printed at this Press in Bodoni type — perhaps rather too elegant a letter for Mr. Canfield's rugged personality, but chosen by Mr. Whitney.

The chief accomplishment of 1930 was the completion of an edition of the revised Book of Common Prayer for which I and three other printers were asked to prepare specimen pages, and for which our pages seemed to the Commission on Revision the most practical. It was an enormous task, and one which taxed our resources in many different directions, but in which what knowledge I had of the history of a Church to which my family have been for nearly three hundred years adherents, and of the liturgical requirements and practical use of the Prayer Book stood me in good stead. The proofs were read not only by our own proof-readers and by those members of the Commission in charge of the work, but also by the readers of the Harvard University Press and of the Riverside Press, Cambridge. The planning of the book was complicated by the fact that from the beginning of Morning Prayer to the end of the Psalter this edition set the pace for all Prayer Books in small format, which by canon law must conform in pagination thereto. Then again, some new features were introduced for which previous books supplied no liturgical precedent, and finally, some solecisms in the typography of the Standard Book of 1892 had to be corrected. The various tables preceding Morning Prayer were the most difficult portion of the book to arrange. In the edition of 1892 these were "boxed" in rules. These rules we did away with, spacing and leading being depended on to separate the figures in the tables from one another. We also induced the Committee to permit the rubrics to be set in roman type printed in red, these directions previously having been set in italic and then rubricated — an unfortunate piece of typographic redundancy. Besides the copies printed on paper, five examples were printed on vellum, and one of these became the "Standard" Book of Common Prayer, which was presented with considerable ceremony to the Convention of the Episcopal Church, sitting at Denver in the autumn of 1931. The expense of the whole undertaking was borne by Mr. J. Pierpont Morgan, who thus repeated his father's generous gift to the Church of the Standard Prayer Book of 1892. Copies were given to the members of the Com-

mission on Revision, to all dioceses and missionary juris-
dictions and their cathedral churches, and to dignitaries of
Churches in communion with the American Church throughout the world. The book was begun in 1928 and was finished
in the autumn of 1930.

Mr. Lawrence C. Wroth, librarian of the John Carter Brown
Library, is the author of a scholarly book entitled *The Colonial Printer*, published by the Grolier Club, New York, and
printed by us in 1931. This very straightforward piece of work
was executed in Mountjoye type, our intention being to make
its typography wholly subservient to Mr. Wroth's text. Like
most Grolier Club publications, this book was issued in a
limited edition at a fairly high price, though it is a pity that
a work so valuable to students is restricted to a class of readers
who seldom have occasion to make practical use of it. In
contrast one may mention the illustrated *Catalogue of the
Exhibited Paintings and Drawings* of the Isabella Stewart
Gardner Museum, Boston, a volume in which much is to be
had at a small price, and (to digress a little) the kind of book
that it is interesting to arrange. There are in this country few
well-printed books at moderate prices, and it is much more of
a feat to produce one than it is to print limited editions at unlimited expense. If this particular catalogue is successful it is
because there were limitations and these limitations were
fairly well surmounted, and yet the cost of the book was kept
at a moderate sum. Compare it with the thirty-dollars-a-copy
limited edition of *Ellen Terry and Bernard Shaw: A Correspondence*, also printed here, and my meaning is obvious.

The outstanding book printed in 1931 was the Latin and
English version of Pope Pius XI's Encyclical Letter on Christian marriage, *Casti Connubii*. This was printed from Bodoni
type, with the Latin text on left-hand pages and the English
version facing it on right-hand pages. The problem here was
to keep the two versions parallel, this being difficult because
Latin is so much more concise than English. It was solved by
beginning a new page at each section of the Pope's letter and
by setting the English translation in italic—a more condensed

letter than roman — and leading it less than the Latin page. The volume is a very Italian affair and was purposely made as Roman as the Prayer Book is Anglican in effect.

The production of the Prayer Book was hampered by a lack of space in which to do the work conveniently, and before the book was finished this was so evident that a change of location, which we had for some time been considering, became a definite necessity. The Press had occupied its Summer Street quarters for some twenty-eight years. When we first moved into them they were considerably beyond our needs. Later we had use for all the space we had; then it became a tight fit; finally, hopelessly congested. We added half a floor to our quarters, but to little purpose, and year by year the work-rooms became more crowded and inconvenient. Our work-people complained of cramped quarters and poor light in exact ratio to the increasing praise of visitors as to the "atmosphere" — attributable chiefly (it may as well be confessed) to the smoke and grime from the South Station directly opposite. But the dirtier the place got the *more* it reminded the romanticist of "the craftsman of the Middle Ages," and the amateur of printing of "some delightful old-world workshop." Finally, after an infinite amount of wearisome search for places that would "do" and of inspection of places that would not, we found at 712 Beacon Street better and larger quarters, and the Press returned to the same street at the other end of which, more than thirty years earlier, it first started out.

AMONG the things I have learned from conducting a press is the importance of efficient co-operation which in industrial establishments is often hampered by a kind of hierarchy. There can be, and often is, in work-shops, a table of precedence — with the result that the office snubs the proof-readers, and the proof-readers the compositors, and the compositors the pressmen, and the pressmen the shippers, and these last insult the office boy, who maltreats the cat because it is the only thing left to which he can be nasty! And, too, when an error is discovered in one department, hours are spent to show that another department is responsible — a game of industrial tag to prove who is "it." In this Press I have remedied this, or think I have done so.

I have also learned the importance of having the office of a press and its work-rooms together. Offices in town and work-rooms elsewhere usually beget perpetual controversy, and points which could be easily solved by conference are relegated to correspondence. An enormous amount of time is wasted by lack of the personal contact which promotes speed in turning out work and good feeling between the work-rooms and the office. The tone of a letter or of even a telephone conversation may be very different in its effect from a face-to-face talk. Often what appears to be the fault of a worker is the result of inadequate instructions from the office or some difficulty the office has not realized, that can be explained in three minutes by the work-man.

For this reason and others it becomes evident that it is best to know personally the people in one's employ. I have been told that this cannot be done in large establishments; but even there, this acquaintance can be extended more widely than is believed. If a man has a thousand employees he perhaps cannot know them all, but he can know some of them, and it is better to know a hundred than none. One reason for this lack of contact is that usually too much power is given to the different foremen, who dismiss and employ on their own initiative and are responsible only to the employer, with whom the work-people have no direct contact and, in some cases, seldom even see. With us the arrangement has been modified; neither in press-room nor in composing-room may the foreman engage help without the applicant's having been seen by Mr. Bianchi or by me, or dismiss help without first consulting us and stating a good reason for doing so. The result of such an arrangement is that the establishment is much more of a unit than when the foremen have unlimited power to engage or dismiss.

It is often as difficult for an employer to enter into the attitude of the worker as it is for the latter to enter into the employer's state of mind. But if, as is sometimes the case, an employer is better educated and has a wider outlook than the man he employs, it is discouraging to discover that when an industrial difficulty arises, and an employee states his position somewhat tactlessly, the employer — forgetting his advantages — becomes as unreasonable as his subordinate. If as a result a matter that might be adjusted ends in a state of unnecessary irritation on both sides, the employer is more at fault than the employee. But my experience has shown me that if a situation is calmly, clearly, simply, and patiently stated, the working-man — when he understands the matter — usually is entirely reasonable.

The difficulties inherent in large establishments can be remedied very simply — by having small ones. And the advantage of that is that the work then shows definite characteristics because the output is controlled by one guiding hand. A good many years ago the late Horace Hart of the Clarendon Press, Oxford, came to see the Press, and looking it over said, "Very interesting, but it will never be very big." To which I replied, "Please God, no." In current typography, the printing one likes for its individuality usually comes from small plants, in which the ideas of the proprietor have not been swamped by the size of his establishment. Small shops do not pay great dividends, but, to quote a distinguished colleague, "It is the wages of life and not the wages of the trade that reward us."

Besides learning something about printing by practicing it, I have also come to perceive that even a modest success brings its penalties. One of these is the incursion of youthful applicants for positions in which they expect to learn how to help us make beautiful books, although admitting complete ignorance of the simplest operations in any department of book-making. Some of them naïvely confess an ultimate intention — after having absorbed whatever we could teach — to set up printing-offices of their own. Others, loving literature, suppose that the making of books (which may or may not contain it) leads to delightful literary associations, and an opportunity to enjoy a book while reading its proofs. As far as I can judge, the unconfessed wish of these young persons is shortly to occupy, in this or some other establishment, the places that Mr. Bianchi and I modestly strive to fill; believing, it would seem, that by a kind of benign contagion they can speedily catch the trick of designing well-made books without knowing how.

Another penalty for a slight proficiency in one's trade is that people become apologetic in presenting little jobs; and by word of mouth and by letter one is asked if one would be "willing to undertake" or "sufficiently interested to do" this or that. Now what a Press needs and wants is work, and there is no reason to appear condescending in accepting it. Over and over we have said that all kinds of work are done here and that no piece of printing, however small, is neglected—much less despised. But this is all to no purpose. "I thought that you only did beautiful work," says the applicant, thereby showing that he thinks beautiful work must look "beautiful" to him, and also incidentally suggesting that standards are being let down in his behalf? The re-iterated statement that labels for biscuit boxes would be a welcome job is supposed to be the amusingly-exaggerated but unconvincing product of a whimsical mind.

As these days of labor have lengthened into years and decades it has become increasingly clear that the beauty of any piece of printing is almost always the by-product of its adaptation to its purpose, that its beauty must be a structural beauty and that ornament, if ornament there be, is only ornamental when allied to its use. In other words, the charm of good printing is something thrown off from its harmonious working. In the visible world we may find an analogy to this if we recognize that, in the charming phrase of Mozley, "all the colors of the landscape, the tints of spring and autumn, the hues of twilight and of dawn—all that might seem the superfluities of Nature, are only her most necessary operations under another view: her ornament is but another aspect of her work: and in the very act of laboring as a machine, she also sleeps as a picture."

53

THIS is the story of the Merrymount Press, and of that segment of my life pertaining thereto. The Press took its name from the fancy that one could work hard and have a good time—which was not true at its beginning, although it has sometimes been since. In no exact sense was the Press ever founded—it only began; and as to its progress—it merely continued. After any venture enjoys for a sufficient number of years a sufficient degree of success, perspective as to its beginnings is gradually lost. What was merely a venture assumes the dignity of a foundation, and its continuance appears to have been a confidently-charted course. Far from being conceived at the outset with a sort of "vision," the Press was begun because of the lack of opportunity in a previous like employment, where the writer was not master but man. Had the difficulties been foreseen, and the likelihood of foundering, rather than of founding, been realized, the project might never have been undertaken at all.

The reason that it has had a measure of success is that it had a sound program which was patiently pursued, i.e. to do the ordinary work of its day well and suitably for the purpose for which it is intended. I have never seen anything amiss with this program, though I have often seen much the matter with the way it was carried out. Nevertheless the effort to get printing "right" led me to collect types and to study them, and to study the history of printing, and finally I began to know something about it, or (as the man said about horses) to "know more than I did." Nearly fourteen thousand pieces of printing of all sorts have been turned out here, and each one of them has had the personal supervision of my partner or myself; and not one but every page of each book has come under our inspection. This means labor, and constant labor; and to such effort—which is within the power of any man— the success of the Press is chiefly due. Add to this a love of order, a wish to make good, and, as a by-product, the desire to demonstrate that a trade can be profitably practiced in the spirit of a profession, and one has the whole story. None of these characteristics or desires has, necessarily, a connection with printing; each is as applicable to other occupations. In this case, through force of circumstances, I happened to apply them to printing, for which I had little taste when I began, nor ever the kind of fervor that is stated (in improving books) to be essential to success. *"Dans toutes les carrières, il existe un conscience du métier,"* said Balzac; and if this conscience is of the New England variety, the result may easily be mistaken for an enthusiastic love of one's calling.

Here my experience as a printer and my record of the Merrymount Press come to an end together. As I cannot know when the inevitable *Finis* will be written against it — or me — instead of saying "The End," I prefer to hope that both are "To be continued." But in looking back over all these years, I still must say with John Clare, "If Life had a second edition, how I would correct the proofs!"

RECOLLECTIONS AND
PERSPECTIVES

STANLEY MORISON

THE death of Daniel Berkeley Updike removed the last and the most widely influential of the notable group of Victorian writers, learned in both the practice and the history of the printing and allied trades, who, together, contributed a body of archeological research and industrial application whose richness and quality must arouse the admiration of future generations. Bibliographical studies in English would be far less advanced than they are today but for the work of Blades, Reed, DeVinne and Updike. But Updike was not an enumerator of editions, an amender of texts or a maker of lists of books printed at this, that, or some other place; he was, rather, a critic with an interest in so much of typographic study as was consistent with an interest in most aspects of style. It is safe to say that he would have felt the same pre-occupation if he had not chosen printing as a professional activity. To begin with he possessed the right endowment and he ended with the broadly-cultivated mind of the accomplished critic. Those who work under the discipline of the art of typography have reason to be grateful for Updike's breadth of view. It distinguishes him from his contemporaries Blades and DeVinne. Comparison with them reveals Updike as almost their equal as an antiquarian, and much their superior as an artist. Appreciation of the aesthetic factor in book-printing cannot be said to be necessary to the enumerator of editions, or to the investigator of texts; it is an essential requirement of the librarian, of the critic, and, certainly, of the fine printer. No doubt Updike's motive for undertaking the research he did was professional, like Blades' and DeVinne's; typographers are fortunate that all three performed so well what they felt as a duty. Not a few problems would otherwise

56

have remained a legacy for investigation by, it can hardly be doubted, writers less gifted than himself. It is a moderate estimate of Updike to say that the combination of judgment, taste, knowledge and thoroughness, not to mention business acumen, that he brought to his chosen work, was rare in his own time and impossible to find in ours. We have no right, at the present stage in the world's affairs, to expect as a mere ordinary dispensation of the nature of things, a second Updike to appear in this generation. It is, moreover, doubtful whether the next generation will find that the line of Blades, Reed, DeVinne and Updike can be extended. For one thing, the old basis of conviction regarding typographical style is in a state of crisis. In Updike's time, the center of the publishing trade passed from his own Boston to a New York that was by no means his own. American books came to be designed and published in an atmosphere that was eclectic whereas Boston was traditionalist; and Updike was himself, in important respects, a traditionalist and proud of it. His taste it may truly be said, had precedents. "Taste" is not genius; it is a faculty not of invention but of discrimination, i.e. between, say, typographical models that deserve consideration. Updike's taste was formed upon a humanistic and traditionalist principle, i.e. "upon the best models." DeVinne's influence upon him was marked. He also owed something to the example of the Chiswick Press of London and the English university presses. It is, however, true that his use of traditional precedents was all his own. He applied them, as precedent deserves to be applied, not by whim but by principle. He respected the past because he regarded wisdom and respected it as the accumulation of the experience of others and a yardstick for the measuring of his own performance. He was a traditionalist for a reason; or, rather, for several reasons.

Daniel Berkeley Updike, the son of Caesar Augustus and Elisabeth Bigelow (formerly Adams) Updike, was born of a family that had for centuries been settled in the neighborhood of Providence. He was an unmistakable Yankee. His father's sudden death deprived him of the means of proceeding with a formal education, but he had already discovered that books were necessary to the furnishing of his life, and volunteered his assistance to the Library of the Providence Athenaeum, where he spent several months. He was glad, at the age of 20, to accept a junior post in the publishing firm of Houghton, Mifflin & Co. of Boston, engaging first in the commercial and publicity departments, and some years later was transferred to the typographical side at the Riverside Press in Cambridge. Updike there showed a capacity for a managing position in the publishing trade, beside an aptitude for the application of sound principles of design to the printed matter under his control. He gave his work most of his energy and though taking time to read, to practice the art of conversation and to exercise his pen, was naturally a man of business. In the New England sense of the term, he was a man likely to do well "in business for himself." Business for Updike was neither an unholy occupation nor a form of amusement. Having chosen printing as his work, he performed it as he thought it should be performed and paid for. His business was never a hobby with him, though dining-out and writing were. He was a charming and solicitous host, a witty talker and an amusing and stylish writer. To be all these things was more important to him than printing. That was his business, his occupation. He felt no need to apologize for taking it sufficiently seriously. But there was in him something more fundamental to his personality. Religion underlay his life and his business; his typographical expression was not at variance with it. He occupied a position half-way between the Laudian High Church and the Oxford Movement presentations of Christianity, and there was nothing easy or spurious, Jacobite or Romanist, about it. The task of living the kind of life he was determined to live did not permit him to shirk difficulties, spiritual, intellectual and other, inherent in that life-long struggle which is the lot of men who take upon themselves, under the grace of God, the burden of self-discipline. The family's long tradition of Episcopalianism was one of the prime sources of his strength of will. There was a touch of

Calvin's austerity in Updike's churchmanship. Love of order, for order's own sake, was second nature to him. Labor, too, was not irksome. "Work hard and have a good time" was one of his principles. He was 33 before he set up, in 1893, under his own name and responsibility, using "The Merrymount Press" as his imprint. Numerous ecclesiastical manuscripts came his way. The most significant work of the period was the *Altar Book*, begun in 1893 and completed in 1896. Large folio in measure, the text of the book was composed in a new roman type designed for the purpose by the architect, Bertram Grosvenor Goodhue, whose churches in the medieval style meet with appreciation even by present-day anti-Goths. I remember with what pleasure Updike described to me the Dominican Church on Lexington Avenue, New York City, and I found much to admire in this specimen of Goodhue's building; not, I venture to think, to be despised by lovers of J. N. Comper. The pages of the *Altar Book* were framed in ornamental borders by Goodhue reminiscent of the Kelmscott style. The decorative initial letters, no two of which are exactly alike, were also the work of Goodhue. Numerous full-page drawings were contributed by Robert Anning Bell. The plain-chant, supervised by Sir John Stainer, is printed with red staves. The whole was rubricated in accordance with the medieval liturgical convention. The pigskin binding was decorated with a blind-stamp design; this, too, by Goodhue.

Updike's office at the time was only equal to the composition of the text, and the pages had to be put to press elsewhere. As only the most accomplished press-work would be acceptable, the whole of the pages, when made up, were dispatched to New York for printing on the presses of De Vinne. The net result is of the greatest interest to any designer occupied with the problems inherent in first-class liturgical typography. Updike's *Altar Book* is a monumental example. It is, in its decorative aspect, certainly a "dated" piece, but the principles of arrangement and display of its text, are none the less instructive. And the credit of this arrangement is wholly Updike's. What he had to learn, and did from DeVinne,

was of a different order. Few were the relevant details of
DeVinne's business practice that the younger man failed to
observe. He noted and respected DeVinne's keen interest in
the historical as well as the technical details of the craft. He
admired DeVinne's habit of going back to the original sources.
But if he had a high opinion of DeVinne's historical knowledge and technical accomplishments, he recognized the limitations of his sense of design and power of typographical
discrimination. Updike's mind on these matters was simpler.
His style was basically English, as DeVinne's was first Italian
and then French. In not a few respects, the Merrymount
Press shows its indebtedness to the late Chiswick Press style
as it had developed under Wilkins and Jacobi. That the two
presses became comparable within twenty years is the measure of Updike's achievement. None of the difficulties was
shirked. How successfully they were solved on a continent
in which the typography of bibliography at that time was
rarely attempted, may be judged from the catalogue of the
John Carter Brown Library. It was a time when the great
Morgan catalogues were composed and printed in England,
generally at the Chiswick Press. The limitations of American
material and skill dictated this course. Updike, with DeVinne,
was a principal contributor to the capacity of American
printers to satisfy the increasing demands of American savants.

A more mature piece of monumental printing than the
Altar Book was the new text of the *Book of Common Prayer*
of the Protestant Episcopal Church, which was printed at the
expense of Mr. J. Pierpont Morgan. Comparison with the
Altar Book of forty years earlier reveals a number of highly
interesting changes in taste. The new text is without decoration other than the accidental allure always imparted to Service
Books by the printing of the rubrics in the correct position and
traditional color. The initial letters are plain, the type is the
seventeenth-century face that was one of three or four peculiar in America, at that time, to the Merrymount Press. These
fonts, following the example of DeVinne, he had collected
in Europe. The discrimination was Updike's own.

In 1903, when he visited Europe, he spent some time in the Printed Books Department of the British Museum, then in its most distinguished period under A. W. Pollard. (It was from Pollard that the present writer first—1916—learnt of Updike's work.) He visited the Kelmscott Press, where he met Sydney Cockerell. Updike also visited Mainz, and proceeded to Leipzig. From the oldest printing office there, that of Drugulin, he purchased fonts of what they correctly called their "Hollandisch" series of romans and italics. In 1914 Updike bought the fonts that have now been identified as Bell's. While these then rare faces were used with consummate skill, the reputation of the Press owed little to the possession of exclusive materials. Updike did not adventure his capital in order to turn typography into something exquisite; but to make it "better for its purpose than was commonly thought worth while." It was task enough for a responsible master-printer, with an organization and a wage bill to meet weekly. The bulk of the Merrymount work, therefore, was composed in such ordinary and, in other hands, generally banal fonts as Caslon and Scotch Roman. Much, if not most of the composition was by hand. Later the Press added Monotype machines to the composing-room. But hand-setting has remained a principal means of conferring distinction upon jobs in which it would be appropriate. In the course of years, the Press had come into the possession of a wide range of historic fonts. The difference between DeVinne's and Updike's collections was fundamental: Updike was not interested in the rare or the curious. His eye was set upon the acquisition of general-purpose fonts.

"Oxford" was the face which, of all those at his command, Updike took most pleasure in using for the class of work for which it was fitted. It is an early nineteenth-century design, transitional between Old Style and Modern. The two-volume work *Printing Types*, which he published in 1922, shows the merits of the type to advantage. It may well be that this book, as significant for the abundant research which it stimulated as for the richness and depth of his own reading, will undoubtedly keep Updike's memory green among later generations of amateurs and professionals who can hardly hope to handle many specimens of his practical typography. The ripeness of judgment as well as the charm and wit of the chapters of *Printing Types* are reflected in the successive phases of Updike's individual use of historic precedents. After the William Morris phase there came the Herbert Horne phase. When, having worked through these sources of inspiration, Updike nourished his mind upon the eighteenth century, he may be said to have "truly found himself." That he was at any time a mere archaist is not true.

Updike's library of books on printing—in the collection of which he was again aided by DeVinne's example,—was a remarkable one. He was, however, dependent upon those precedents that reached back to more than a generation. Updike's last publication, *Some Aspects of Printing Old and New*, was printed in 1941 in the Times New Roman. He was the first in America to procure this font. The volume contained some lectures that he had delivered at the Huntington Library, a great adventure for one who had traveled so little in the United States. He flew out to the coast for this purpose, and, as he told me in a letter, thoroughly enjoyed the experience, and was delighted with the people. Later, finding himself in need of a change, he went to Guatamala by airplane. He was 80 at the time, and in full vigor. He maintained his attendance at the office and also at the meetings of the Boston Club of Odd Volumes. There was, it would seem, nothing to stop him. But the events of 1938 and 1939 took a heavy toll. When war came to Europe it brought a continual and catastrophic interruption to Updike's peace of mind. In his last year he confessed, in a letter to me, to a sense of paralyzing spiritual weariness he had never before experienced. Nevertheless, he strove by his letters to encourage his English friends. He had a very clear idea of what the war was about and felt no need in 1939 to apologize for it to his compatriots. His end came suddenly, three weeks after Pearl Harbor.

I last heard from him in November 1941, from his business

address and still in harness. He had then taken a lot of trouble to give me details of a certain printing problem we were both interested in. It must have been in the summer of 1924 that I first made his personal acquaintance, at a country place he then had beyond North Adams. This was during my first visit to the United States. I went as a pilgrim, for the two volumes of *Printing Types* had been published in 1922. No more need be said here than that this publication was the most exciting event of a decade. Its value to a country that had been starved of typographical literature since 1914 can hardly be imagined by Americans. To us at that time the book had a messianic quality. Despite the immense amount of research that has been done since, and which Updike's work was designed to inspire, *Printing Types* remains absolutely essential to the understanding of the subject; and, as far as the intelligent appreciation of printing style is concerned, every bit as valuable today as it was twenty years ago. The book, like the man I met, was not made in a hurry. It is worth recalling that *Printing Types* was based on lectures given between 1911 and 1916. Upon some sections Updike had worked and thought for 10 years, before committing himself to print. His chapters on the great French typographical dynasties of Fournier and Didot and his Spanish section exhibit marked originality and independence. The whole is a combination of charm, wit and solidity.

The man I discovered was rather below than above middle height, spare in frame, neat in appearance, positive in expression. As on many occasions since, he proved a most agreeable host. To me a habit of routine made him the pleasantest person to be with. It would have been, I guessed, more than difficult — impossible rather — either for himself or anybody else to break his continuity of practice, the pattern and framework of his exterior life. He was, I judged, immovably attached to the virtues of self-reliance, hard work, and thrift which were so intensively cultivated in Old and New England when he was a boy, of which less and less has been heard both sides of the ocean during the past twenty-five years. I recognized at once, too, that Updike was very deeply rooted in the spiritual department of life, besides the social, professional, and commercial. Nothing he seemed to say or do was done rashly; nor was there any precipitancy in making what this generation calls "contacts." Similarly, Updike was too surely what spiritual writers describe as a "recollected" man to allow conversation to degenerate into mere gossip. In his relish for talk about persons as well as things he was careful to refrain from harsh verdicts upon men as men. But he had too good an eye for genuine quality to be patient under any attempt to secure his approval of work that was pretentious, showy or egoistic. His comments then, however acid in form, were never spiteful in substance. He showed, in fact, an unexpected keenness of sight in searching for redeeming qualities and a tenderness towards those the Victorians called the "deserving" poor. All these characteristics he had, I came to think, regulated into a pattern of life from which he had no desire to stray. He was himself the center of the pattern and he might have lost in humanity but for his religion, his humor and his reading.

Updike had an immense respect for learning, but a horror of pedantry. It amused him that the partial reference in *Printing Types* to his superb collection of typographical documents should have led the book-sellers to commend specimens he had not chosen to mention, with the rubric "Not in Updike." I have never known a collector more judicious or one less given to bibliomania, a printer whose work was more admirable, or a scholar who carried his learning more easily.

When I began to know Updike he was already over sixty and had experienced so much that, to a man of his acute powers of observation both of himself and others, any tendency to rashness of appreciation or the reverse had long been suppressed. If he could be severe with others, he was certainly severe with himself, having that merciless self-scrutiny of his motives and his work which is the necessary preliminary to the making of an artist. He had the endowment to have succeeded in literature had he chosen and from time to time threw off amusing squibs in prose and verse.

I never had much talk with Updike about professional affairs. Our conversation turned rather to religious matters. We had both read widely in theology, and both felt keenly the intellectual and the moral difficulties in all institutional religion. When I first knew him he perhaps insisted rather upon the points which separated us, but in later years he would accompany me to Mass in a rather poky, not to say dirty, Catholic Church in Boston of his own choice, which I cannot now identify.

My diary and his letters were destroyed in the great raid of May 10th, 1941, and I cannot now be sure of the date of my last sight of him. It was in the early weeks of the year of fate, 1939. I sought him one evening in his office in the Beacon Street building. On the way out something was wrong with the lift. We were compelled to walk, and I could not help admiring the voiceful and masterful way in which he dealt with the delinquent. We left the office, crossed the road in the teeth of a fierce wind sweeping round through Kenmore Square. We were, I considered, lucky to find a cab on the rank. Updike opened the door of one, only to find the driver inside, taking refuge from the cold. This, possibly, might have been excused. But the man was smoking. "I have said to you before," he was sharply told, "that I will not take your cab after you have been smoking in it," and then his door was banged upon him. Fortunately another cab drove on to the rank, whose driver, lacking the occasion of sin, was commissioned to drive to Updike's new and extremely suitable house on Marlborough Street, where he had plenty of room. I greatly enjoyed seeing him so handsomely and comfortably installed. All his life, it had seemed to me, he had avoided so much comfort. Our talk was mainly political. I had been delivering lectures at the Metropolitan Museum, New York, and had visited friends at Washington and Chicago, at all of which places I had been under the necessity of doing my best with the apparent "yellowness" of Chamberlain's "appeasement" policy. I found Updike just as interested in the international situation and rather more gloomy than I expected. He was even more gloomy about the American domestic situation. That was not unexpected. He had no more use for a New Deal than a New Gospel. He felt uneasy as I did. I promised to proceed as quickly as possible with the work, already begun, upon a volume of my collected papers, to which he was to contribute an introduction.

Had Updike lived another eight weeks he would have been 82 years of age; and had completed half a century at the Merrymount Press. His mature work, accomplished after he was 45, has a quality that is rarer than style. He was 50 when he began the series of lectures that formed the basis of *Printing Types*. These two historical volumes, like his practical work, have character. This is not the place in which to compare these volumes, published in 1922, with DeVinne's *Plain Printing Types* published in 1899, and other works. But DeVinne also was a character. Both men produced a body of work that is consistent with itself and with exigent personal standards, based in their separate and contrasting approach to typographical history and practice.

The essential qualities of the work of the Merrymount Press, i.e. accurate composition of the text; occasional decoration; proportionate and therefore satisfactory imposition; scrupulous presswork; careful folding, sewing and wrapping of the finished product, may be said without exaggeration or disrespect to DeVinne, to have reached a higher degree of quality and consistency than that of any other printing-house of its size, and period of operation, in America or Europe.

HAND-BOOK FOR AN EXHIBITION

GREGG ANDERSON

ALTHOUGH D. B. Updike began his work in 1893 under the influence of William Morris, his later development was in a different direction. Instead of producing books with a purely aesthetic appeal—the purpose of Morris—Updike soon made it his concern to see that the books he printed were first of all readable and suited to the conditions under which they would be used; and then, when these requirements had been met, that their style was within the standards of good taste which he had set for himself, after a thorough study of the best printing of the past. The measure of his success in solving these problems of printing, and the correctness of his approach to them, have grown more apparent as the years have passed. Instead of printing books of interest only to collectors, the Merrymount Press has served an ever-increasing number of customers in the different fields of learnings, until it is now numbered among the leading scholarly presses of this country.

Updike once remarked that he himself was not a practical printer and that he could not set type or lock up a form. In that narrow sense, Updike could not be called a printer. But in the larger sense of the word, by his control of the work and by his direction of the organization producing it, he has every claim to be considered one of the few well-rounded, complete printers. There are several requirements to be met by the complete printer, and Updike was successful in meeting them.

Perhaps of most importance in the list of qualifications of the ideal printer are a scholarly mind and a methodical disposition. These would be clearly reflected in the style of printing and also in the proof-reading standards. Another essential is a knowledge of the history and development of printing, which brings acquaintance with the many conventions relat-

67

ing to the making of books. Still another necessity is a sense of craftsmanship, with an understanding of the machinery to be used and the way in which it is to be controlled. To supplement this craftsmanship, which would be constantly striving for a better and more refined product, there should be a critical and discriminating mind to insure distinctive work. Moreover, the press itself must be conducted on a businesslike basis. The work must be delivered when promised, the customer assured of competent fulfillment of his requirements, and all details well attended to. Finally, the printer is under obligations, both to his fellow-printers and to the citizens of his community, to broaden the scope of his field by overcoming its limitations; to uphold the best practices of the craft; and to contribute as much of his time and effort as can be spared toward better relations and better understanding between printers and the general public.

In each of these respects, the Merrymount Press has excelled. There have been presses and printers that were, perhaps, more able in some one direction than this Press has been, but few, in any age, that have ranked as high in all of them. Many of the private presses have concentrated so completely on the quality of their work that they have disregarded the necessity of being able to sell it. There have been other printers who have developed large and profitable businesses, but have been unable to maintain a uniformly high quality of product. The Merrymount Press has neither slighted the quality of its work, nor overlooked the need of satisfying its customers.

The contributions of Bianchi to the soundness and financial stability of the firm are many. He has long been responsible for all estimating, a very important part of any printing-office. Noteworthy, also, is the fact that the Press' cost system and job-order numbering date from 1915, the year in which he became a partner. Updike, in his *Notes on the Merrymount Press,* and elsewhere, acknowledged his own difficulty with figures. The combination of his taste and knowledge and Bianchi's thorough craftsmanship and good business head was a satisfactory and congenial one.

The Press, even in its busiest days, has seldom employed more than thirty people at any time — not a large number, as businesses go in this country. However, if the organization had been much larger, Updike would necessarily have had to delegate part of the task of designing to others, which would have meant books other than those for which he was personally responsible. He said that practically every proof for every book produced at the Press passed through his hands or those of his partner.

In a business sense a printing-plant which one man can control is a workable and economical unit. The competent printer must bring to bear such intangibles as his intelligence, taste, education, precision, and understanding of his customers' wants. Obviously, he can not delegate successfully what he alone can do.

In a shop with a moderate amount of business, there is not apt to be so much fluctuation as in a big shop; the creation of a special sales department is not necessary; nor is it essential to have the wide variety of equipment (including, as a rule, some which is unprofitable) called for by the greater diversification of large volume. The plant of medium size is usually more consistently profitable over a period of time than the larger one, all things being equal. So the deliberately restricted size of the Press has been good business and has also assured the high quality of work possible with one-man control.

Naturally, control must be intelligent. Updike's familiarity with the history of printing and with the great printers and books of the past — a familiarity demonstrated in his book, *Printing Types* — was the result of many years of study. This background, re-inforced by a discriminating taste, helped him to make use of the best in the way of type and ornament from earlier days and gave him standards by which to judge and select from newer types, papers, and ornaments. The books of the Press are illustrations of the importance to a printer of a knowledge of the finest examples of printing.

Updike's books and articles about printing are another facet of his achievement. He wrote with distinction, and his works

are as notable, in their way, as is his printing. He had a retentive memory and was able to recall and effectively quote
extracts from other writers. His writing was carefully done—
sparkling, clear, and to the point. Apart from his two-volume
Printing Types, his books are small, but *In the Day's Work*
and *Some Aspects of Printing,* though short, are important.
He is also the author of *Richard Smith, First English Settler
of the Narragansett Country,* and edited *A Dissertation upon
English Typographical Founders and Founderies,* by Edward
Rowe Mores. Of particular interest is his *Notes on the Merrymount Press and Its Work,* which includes a list, compiled by
Julian Smith, of the books printed at the Press. An urbane
and completely charming summing-up of Updike's experience
as a printer, the book is an ideal introduction to the man and
his work.

An outstanding quality of Updike was his restraint. Sham
or pretense of any sort was anathema to him. He had no illusions about his own work and took no comfort from praise
by the ignorant. Although inclined to be reticent, he had a
sharp tongue and pen, and could protect himself capably from
over-aggressiveness or any attempt to impose on his time or
good nature. He said, "I have learned if people push, to push
back." But, barring this slight acidity, he was rather shy and
of a sensitive nature.

During his lifetime, he did a vast amount of plain hard work.
Perhaps because he realized how much he put into each production of the Press, he was impatient with amateurs or dilettantes who thought that inspired work was effortless. He was
an infallibly prompt letter writer, and he lost no time in
applying himself to any and every task he undertook.

Updike was a willing contributor to efforts toward the
progress of the craft. He was one of the founders of the
Society of Printers in Boston, and through the years gave
freely of his time and energy in furthering its projects. He
was not overly fond of group activities in general, and was
inclined to avoid organization meetings and activities of a
pseudo-social nature; but he was always most willing to lend

his support to genuine efforts toward the improvement of printing.

Respected and honored by his fellow-printers, and by that part of the general public interested in the printing of books, Updike examplified in his career the result of "an intensive cultivation of the field that is given a man to till"—to use his own words. When that intensive cultivation is joined with knowledge, taste, and integrity of purpose, the work produced can hardly fail to be distinguished.

Updike's example has served to light the way for many printers. The qualities demonstrated so successfully in his books have perceptibly raised printing standards. His example has shown that printing, instead of making few demands on those engaged in it, actually makes many, if it is to be done well. D. B. Updike, in his work, dignified his trade, as he dignified himself, by the manner in which he practiced it.

THE BOOKS OF THE MERRYMOUNT PRESS

I. ECCLESIASTICAL PRINTING

THE ecclesiastical printing done by the Press is a good demonstration of the superior results to be obtained from a trained and intelligent approach to a problem. Updike had long been a member of the Episcopal church, and had acquired a most useful knowledge of church history and ecclesiastical forms. Able to understand the value of restraint and propriety as applied to daily life, he was equally able to understand the value and use of the forms set for printing of a religious nature. Working within that pattern, he infused it with a dignity and beauty in keeping with the subject.

Naturally, the freedom and variety shown in some of the other books is not to be found here. The bindings are severely plain. There is seldom any ornament, except when the influence of William Morris is apparent, in the early years of the Press' ecclesiastical printing. Red is employed, but only in accordance with ecclesiastical usage.

In spite of these restrictions, the 1930 edition of the Book of Common Prayer — simple, handsome, of the best materials, and intelligently planned and carefully executed — is one of the finest achievements of the Press and an outstanding example of American printing at its best. Three other printers, one from the United States and two from England, were also invited to submit plans for the edition, but almost anyone comparing the four specimens prepared would agree that the committee was wise in choosing that of the Merrymount Press.

Two books might be mentioned to indicate the designer's consciousness of his problem. *The Order of Evening Worship* is a comparatively small book set in a type somewhat larger than might have been expected. A note in the book, stating that services were held by candlelight, helps one to understand that choice of type. Another book, *Pius XI on Christian Marriage*, presented the problem of keeping the Latin and English versions (printed on facing pages) parallel. The difficulty came from the fact that Latin is much more concise than English. The solution was to set the English text in italic, a more condensed letter than roman, and to use less leading between the lines. Then, by starting a new page at each section of the Pope's letter in order to even up any remaining variations, the problem was solved.

Unless we know all about the printing of a book — or the making of anything — we are not apt to appreciate how many obstacles have to be surmounted to produce the finished result. We think, in the instance just mentioned: "Isn't it pleasant that the Latin and English should come out on facing pages," without realizing the work involved in making that possible. But one may be sure that any book which is simple, readable, and easy to use and to understand, did not just happen so. Simplicity, clarity, and directness are not easily realized. They come only after the clearing away and weeding out of the unnecessary, and they indicate a mastery of medium that only a few printers achieve.

II. TRADE PUBLICATIONS

As a first consideration in discussing the trade books produced by the Merrymount Press, it is well to fix in mind the time at which most of them were printed. In 1902 the Press produced forty-one books, of which nineteen were for trade publishers. In 1914 twenty books were produced, ten of them for institutions and only one for a trade publisher.

The assumption that the early years of the Press were devoted chiefly to trade books is correct. Publishers in the late 1890's and early 1900's, when public interest in printing was relatively high, found Updike's work decorative, colorful, and salable; and orders multiplied. The subsequent change to simpler design was probably one reason for the decrease in the amount of trade printing. Another might well have been the fact that publishers did not care to continue to spend extra money for such printing after the novelty wore off.

Updike says of some of the Press' early printing: "As I look back upon this body of work, I wonder why I worked so hard on it, and why, having worked so hard on it, I haven't done it better." Of course, the answer is that no one does his best without a preliminary period of trial and error. These books were the proving-ground that preceded the Press' later success in various fields.

As any flourishing business must, the Press made stepping-stones of its successive books. One well-done piece of printing usually led to the placing of other orders by the publisher or author for whom the work was done. Thus, many volumes were printed for T. Y. Crowell & Co. Edith Wharton, a personal friend, recommended the Press for the printing of her books, and business relations with Charles Scribner's Sons over a considerable period resulted.

A list of the publishers who ordered printing in those first years would include most of the leading firms in the country — among them, T. Y. Crowell & Co.; R. H. Russell; Dodd, Mead & Co.; Charles Scribner's Sons; D. Appleton and Co.; L. C. Page and Co.; Longmans, Green & Co.; D. C. Heath & Co.; Doubleday, Page and Co.

As a group the trade books are the least interesting of the Press' output. As already indicated, they were done, in the majority of cases, during the early years of the Press, when its work was less competently handled than later. Moreover, these books do not, as a rule, call for the care and skill that must go into those in the other classes. The text ordinarily presents fewer problems, and cheaper materials are used. Because of the wider audience, the tendency is toward simplicity, little decoration, and no eccentricities that might confuse. Some of the trade publications were of considerable size. *The Life and Works of Charles Lamb*, for the Pafraets Book Company, was in twelve volumes. For R. H. Hinkley Co. was printed an edition of the Bible in fourteen volumes, and for the same firm an edition of the works of John Milton in four volumes.

In spite of the fact that most of the trade printing was done in the days of the Press' youth, books for trade publishers have continued to appear. Nowadays, however, few of them are for the large publishing houses. Most of the work in recent years for such customers has been in the form of limited-edition printing.

III. PRIVATELY-PRINTED BOOKS

A PRIVATELY-PRINTED book is one produced for distribution by the author or some other interested person who defrays the cost of printing, and who issues the work without offering it for public sale. Fairly often books privately printed are of a personal nature—family records or family histories of little general interest. They may be pieces printed for special occasions, or intended by donors for particular groups.

The books in this class are naturally less formal than those intended for the general public or a wider audience. Many of the privately-printed books have striking bindings, decorative title-pages, or color on text pages. Frequently, it is possible to print them on much better paper than could be afforded for books to be placed on public sale.

A large quantity of private printing implies a social class
with money enough for such purposes, with sufficient interest
in its family backgrounds and in its friends to go to the expense
involved, and with an awareness and taste sufficiently developed to appreciate a nicety like design in books. New
England, in general, meets these requirements, and, as D. B.
Updike had many years of social contacts there, much of the
work naturally gravitated to him.

The variety and ingenuity shown in some of the privately-
printed books deserve comment. Only a printer can realize the
effort required to resist the inertia of printing books to a
pattern. Only a printer, too, can appreciate the difficulties
imposed by the twin pressures of having to get the work out
on time and at an estimated cost. Both these factors discourage
experimentation or unusual treatment but Updike nevertheless succeeded in designing each book individually, keeping
clearly in mind its contents and use. For example, compare the
dainty, elegant little volume of poems, *Pierrot's Verses*, issued
by a woman for her friends, with the large and impressive
Sulgrave Manor *Record*, a book intended to commemorate a
group of donors and to be placed in the libraries of the spon-
soring organization's chapters in the various states. Are these
not right treatments of two very different problems?

The other books in the group illustrate the same awareness
of subject matter, and the same ability to present it in pleasing
form. The titles which contain letters or reminiscences of
earlier days are suitably clothed — typography, as well as text,
echoes the past. But always there is a clear, readable page, and
never does the treatment do more than harmonize with the
author's words.

IV. LIMITED EDITIONS AND BOOK-CLUB PUBLICATIONS

ANOTHER class of books produced successfully by the Press
has been publications for book clubs and limited editions for
trade publishers. Work of this sort is a very direct challenge
to the printer's skill, since the purchaser of a limited edition,

or the member of a bibliophile club, usually has more than an ordinary interest in printing. Such buyers, able to appreciate niceties, have long been numbered among the collectors of Merrymount Press items.

This group, more than any other, represents the printer's work when he has a comparatively free hand. Whereas in the case of privately-printed books the ideas of the customer are bound to make themselves felt, here the printer is expected only to turn out a handsome and well-made product. The books are usually sold at higher prices than are charged for trade books, a minimum amount being reserved for the costs of distribution, and a maximum set aside for actual printing. The paper can be, and often is, of superior or, indeed, the best quality; frequently, a hand-made sheet can be selected. It is possible to make additional printings, adding color for decoration, and in the choice of type to use more decorative letters than are normally employed. Also, the binding can be of better grade, with perhaps more emphasis on appearance and less on durability.

Updike was one of the first American printers to produce period books. His knowledge of printing history, in conjunction with his taste, made him aware of the fitness of giving an eighteenth-century text a flavor of eighteenth-century printing; and many of the most charming books in the privately-printed group as well as in the limited editions would fall into this category. Updike's knowledge of type and ornament naturally led to his purchase of the best from the past, so that in his work he was able to select appropriate ornaments, decorations, and styles of type.

A series of books issued by the Merrymount Press under the title of *The Humanists' Library* illustrates a venture into limited-edition publishing. The books, according to Updike, sold out; but evidently the series was not a complete success, because after the eighth volume—*A Renaissance Courtesy-Book,* issued in 1914—no more were printed. For their time, they were satisfactory enough and on a par with the books of the private presses that flourished during the 1890's and 1900's. All of these Merrymount items are attractive but they do not represent the high quality which we now associate with the Press.

Among the artists who have contributed decorations to the books of the Press, three in particular — T. M. Cleland, W. A. Dwiggins, and Rudolph Ruzicka — have been especially skillful in combining their talents with those of the printer. Their connections with the Press began fairly early: Cleland's in 1903, Dwiggins' in 1908, and Ruzicka's in 1912. Each collaborated successfully to produce a harmonious result in the finished book. Ruzicka, notably in the series of annual keepsakes done for the Press since 1912, has created some of America's most distinguished wood-engravings in color. The book *Newark*, for which he contributed black as well as colored engravings, is one of the many handsome volumes graced by his work. Another extremely charming example is La Fontaine's *Fables*, for which he supplied a series of delicately sharp and clear little engravings.

W. A. Dwiggins has also produced many attractive decorations for Merrymount books. As Dwiggins himself acknowledges in his article in *The Fleuron*, he owes much to the discipline and good taste of Updike. A particularly happy achievement of the two was the edition of Walton's *Compleat Angler*, published by Goodspeed. T. M. Cleland, likewise, has made a distinct contribution. Because of his ability to capture the style of any period, he has been unusually clever in adapting his work to text and format, and his fine craftsmanship has enriched many Merrymount volumes. *Benvenuto Cellini* and *A Renaissance Courtesy-Book* are two conspicuous examples. Of late, other demands have reduced the amount of work Dwiggins and Cleland have been able to do for the Press, but Ruzicka has continued to supply a number of illustrations each year. Their quiet charm, and the competent quality of their engraving, have been particularly at home in the setting contributed by the Merrymount Press books.

V. LEARNED AND INSTITUTIONAL PRINTING

OF THE several kinds of books produced at the Press, the publications for colleges and universities, libraries and museums, and learned societies, make up what is perhaps the most important group. Not until about 1910, some seventeen years after the establishment of the Press, did the output in this class become considerable. Such work demands the most exacting attention in its production. Not only must the utmost care be taken in the proof-reading, but the press must also be able to reproduce the illustrative material often included, take care of composition in foreign languages if need be, and set complicated matter. In addition, the choice of types and the design should be carried out in good taste and in a manner in keeping with the subject.

Naturally, the bindings will be plain and durable. There will be little or no ornament, since these books are utilitarian — to be used for their content rather than to be admired for their external appearance. In common with the ecclesiastical publications, the scholarly books must conform to a pattern developed through many years. The printer's familiarity with that pattern and his ability to use the scholarly conventions to the best advantage in making the text intelligible, are very soon apparent.

These books, because of the problems which they present, were of particular interest to Updike. While it is not necessary that the printer be completely familiar with the text of the author, no matter what the subject, nevertheless he must understand in general the way in which the author wants the material presented and he must interpret in type the intention of the author. As Updike so often said in his writings about printing, the problem and its solution were of much more interest to him than any other single feature in connection with the production of the books. Museum catalogues, for example, of necessity priced within the means of the casual visitor, were apt to be far more of a challenge to him than a privately-printed volume whose price was subject to no such restriction.

It was in some respects an advantage to Updike that his knowledge of the details of the trade was not so complete as that of a man who had worked at the actual production of books. A proof-reader whose task was to make the corrections in type that he marked might, after a time, tend to reduce their number by consciously or unconsciously weighing the importance of the correction against the amount of work involved. On the other hand, Updike, not being involved in the mechanics of printing, did not allow his critical faculties to be over-ruled by practical considerations of time and expense. Bianchi, in successfully and thoroughly attending to the details of production, gave Updike freedom to plan the work and see that it was done properly.

One quality immediately apparent in Updike's books is his orderliness. Both his home and his office reflected this quality. He continually occupied himself with gathering up and putting away whatever might have got out of place. Much of his delight in the satisfactory solution of some problem connected with printing a book came from his sense of order, and its application to what he was doing.

Updike's energy in getting work done was also an invaluable asset to him. His ability to see a book whole from the beginning, to spend the required time on the different elements involved during its production, to slight nothing, leave no loose ends, was remarkable. The fact that all the books show equal care is as much a tribute to his dogged persistence as to his good judgment and good taste. He respected work and knew its value, because he had learned from experience how great a part of any accomplishment it is.

For thirty-three years the Press has produced annually the Report of the Carnegie Foundation for the Advancement of Teaching, and its work for Brown University covers a period almost as long. The mere fact that the connection of the firm with these two institutions has thus persisted is evidence of satisfactory relations. The Carnegie reports, as well as the different catalogues done for Brown, are models of skill in intricate composition. Moreover, the Carnegie reports of later years show in handling and design considerable change and improvement as compared with the first of the series.

There has been similar improvement in almost all of the productions of the Press—an indication of a right approach in the beginning and a steady progress through the years.

The fact that the Merrymount Press has remained in existence nearly half a century while doing work of the highest quality bespeaks the business judgment and executive ability of the men in charge. Through wars and depressions it has continued on its course because it has offered a service valued by scholars and businessmen alike.

A TRIBUTE TO
DANIEL BERKELEY UPDIKE

T. M. CLELAND

THERE is nothing so poignantly regrettable in the course of human relationships as that the full measure of their value is rarely revealed to us until death has put an end to them. It is a welcome assignment indeed to be asked to write some words of tribute to my late friend, Daniel Berkeley Updike, and one that I should be reluctant to forego in view of my affectionate regard and grateful memory of him. But the sudden revelation of his true import to me and to the world in which he lived and worked that has come with his departure from it, makes it seem an undertaking beyond my reach. To write impersonally, after a friendship of more than forty-two years, and under so great a debt to him as I am, both cultural and moral, would be impossible.

It is no easy matter to state briefly or clearly what I believe to be the particular quality of Updike's part in that renaissance of interest in the improvement of printing in which he was engaged for more than half a century. But it is easy to say, without fear of contradiction, that no influence in all that time has been as important, or any contribution more substantial than his. Starting his career as a printer in what is now referred to as the "gay nineties," he was, as we all were then, awakened and impressed with the idea of printing as an art, by the monumental talent and medieval craftsmanship of William Morris. But he was the first, I believe, to recover from what we all now recognize as the sentimental aspects of that heroic movement, and to perceive through his innate common sense that the making of books which were fifteenth-century *objets d'art*, however beautiful in themselves, did not solve the problem of readable printing for our age, any more than crenelated walls, slit-like windows, and massive oaken furniture would advance a much-needed reform in suburban domestic architecture.

I have two little books, one from the Riverside Press, dated 1896, and another under the imprint of the Merrymount Press, circa 1898, which both exhibit symptoms of the early Morris influence. Both are tastefully and carefully executed within their somewhat overly-elaborate gothic style. The latter is a collection of essays by Dr. Henry van Dyke, called *Ships and Havens,* and its highly rubricated ecclesiastical aspect appears to have no other warrant than that its author was a clergyman! This is, as nearly as I can imagine, what Updike might have said of it himself in later years. In singular contrast to these, and dated only two years later, is another little book of verses, by A. S. Hardy, printed for Scribner's — the first specimen of his work he ever gave me. Set in the sober "Scotch" type which he was the first to use in this country, it is an early example of the unadorned simplicity, the strict dependence upon carefully-composed and tastefully-arranged typography alone, which became the basis of his style thereafter. He did not object to ornament — in fact he delighted in using it and had the keenest sense of its style, its scale, and its relationships that I have ever encountered in anyone. He understood perfectly its functions in printing and reserved it for those special cases where it might enhance and not disturb the usefulness of the thing printed.

But it may be said that his first, and perhaps most important, contribution to the revival of printing as an art, was that he rescued it in its adolescence from a trend toward romantic archaism and much else that was sentimental and silly, and directed the impulse in the direction of practical application and common sense. Resolutely, and without compromise, he held it upon this course. Through research and scholarship he discovered standards for himself which he has in turn set for others; and if at the moment there are few who have the capacity or the sense to follow them, the standards will still be there for the guidance of future generations.

It should be remembered that those qualities of assured

taste and practicality which are so obvious to us today were not always understood as such in the beginning, but were often mistaken by the complacently ignorant for artistic affectation. An anecdote I have always been fond of illustrates the attitude of the "practical" printers of the days when the Merrymount was a Press in name only, and was obliged to have its press-work done by other establishments. Entering one of these which was then very successful, but now quite forgotten, Updike sent in his card and was greeted by the foreman who, studying the card, said: "Updike . . . Updike. Oh, you're the fellow who does the queer printing, aren't you?" "Perhaps," said Updike, "but will you permit me to remind you that *your* printing looks as queer to me as *mine* possibly can to you?" His wit was always the by-product of clear thinking and the needle-sharp focus of his mind. In a letter of many years ago, I find this: ". . . it is truthful, and truth often has the appearance of wit to those unaccustomed to deal with it." He had tolerance and kindness toward all who tried to understand, however falteringly; but his razor wit could sever the head of a fool so deftly and so quietly withal, that the fool would never miss it.

It is impossible to dissociate the works of men of the first order from their personalities because creative work of any kind, to be first-rate, must be the living expression of the personality and character of its creator. This is especially true of Updike, whose printed pages reflect so perfectly the quality of his mind and even of his speech. One is tempted to speculate upon the question of whether a man with less command of his language could give that language printed form as beautifully as he did. It is undeniable that back of all outstanding work in so highly specialized a field there must be a great and varied store of things which do not appear on the surface of the work itself. There is always to be found behind the achievement of even a minor perfection, some universality of interest and culture.

Updike — self-educated — brought to his work a cultivation and scholarship that was authentic in the purest sense — that

83

which is a growth from within, and not merely a private intellectual museum of acquired *belles lettres* and *objets d'art*. His taste and sense of form grew, to be sure, throughout his lifetime; but I cannot imagine him at any age, from the cradle on, entirely without them. His orderliness of mind sprang from a deep instinct and was manifest in everything he did. One of my earliest impressions was of his nervous susceptibility to objects out of place. He would start up in the midst of a conversation to straighten something on the mantlepiece, and a picture on the wall, ever so little off the horizontal, tortured him. This congenital sensitivity of the artist accounts for the perfection of his literary style as well as his printed work; he had for both the same acute perception, the same intolerance of flaws. He was not a writer by profession, but had he been, there are few men living who could have matched his style. I have never seen anything he wrote that was not worth reading; but certain of his things should be classed as "required" by all aspiring printers. *Printing Types* for one — the classic work that marks him as a scholar of the first order — or if not all of it, at very least the Introduction and Conclusion. The highly practical as well as entertaining essays grouped under the title *In the Day's Work* for another, and his last published work, *Some Aspects of Printing Old and New*. The two pages at the end of this book, prophetically titled "A Last Word" sum up his philosophy of living, and of dying, well, and they could be read with profit by every troubled mind in this shattered world today.

Because it is in the nature and spiritual circumstances of some men to develop best within the confines of faith and creed, he retained throughout his life a sincerely devotional religious spirit. It was not such as to hamper the free growth of his intellect or destroy his liberality toward those who did not share his convictions — it commanded their respect. Nor did it ever dull his irrepressible sense of humor — the infallible diagnostic of true intelligence. It was this which lightened and lent grace to all he said and wrote. It can even be sensed in much of his work. In conversation, in the treasure of letters that I have from him, in his words that are printed and published, he made use of his wit to convey sober wisdom, philosophic precept, and even, as in *Printing Types*, cold historic facts. In this as in much else, he was essentially a product of the eighteenth century. Of his own deeply sensitive reaction to the beauties of nature, he could write to me during his last autumn in Vermont: "The trees are tiresomely resplendent — they give one no peace!"

It was there in the quiet contours of the Vermont hills, at the pleasantly rural retreat he had made for a part of each year, that I saw him for the last time. I did not believe then that it was the last time, because I could discover no mark of age in him unless it were an increase in his natural kindliness. His mind was as keen and as sharply tuned to reason as it had ever been, his wit as breath-taking in its speed. In reply to my letter remarking this he wrote: "No, I suppose I have not changed much — I often wish I could or had. It is not much fun being 'me.' However, one has one's uses which are not promoted by fussing about oneself." Such was the patient humility of a truly great man's approach to his mortal end. Never physically robust, and handicapped by many other circumstances in early life; entering his vocation, as he declared, purely by accident; he yet contrived to make of it and himself, through courage, self-discipline, and uncompromising integrity, a still living and radiant example.

UPDIKE OF MERRYMOUNT
THE SCHOLAR-PRINTER

M. A. DE WOLFE HOWE

THE names of the Merrymount Press and of Daniel Berkeley Updike, who died in Boston near the end of 1941, almost eighty-two years of age, are inseparably connected. They suggest first of all to many who know them the production of beautiful books, both ecclesiastical and secular, often sumptuous and costly. It is nevertheless a fact that one of the last undertakings of the Merrymount Press in Updike's lifetime was the printing of a general time-table for the Boston and Maine Railroad. In a time of curtailment of many plans this was not carried beyond the making of an *Index to Tables*, a list of all the stations on all the branches of the road. It takes no expert knowledge of typography to see at a glance that this Index, in the current B.&M. folders, is an object of real beauty attained through clarity. At the very beginning of Updike's career as a printer he declared his aim "to make work better for its purpose than was commonly thought worth while." There spoke an intensely practical realist who felt that print was intended first and foremost to be read, and was glad to undertake any and every form of printing, from folios of learning to advertising cards, so long as he could do it in his own way. Because he was also an artist and a scholar, deeply imbued with a sense of the fitness of things, he brought to his work a capacity for which "unique" does not seem too strong a term.

Now it is the achievement of Updike in his chosen field of printing, whether of stately tomes or of timetables, that makes him a figure of public interest and justifies such a paper as this. Let it be said at once that he could never have achieved what he did had he not been essentially a perfectionist—a devotee to what seemed the very best in his eyes, an embodi-

86

ment of a pet word of my own, "aristophile." A family motto, *Optimum vix satis,* used for his own book-plate, spoke for his feeling that the best was hardly enough, in whatever field. He used it also for a colophon in the first substantial book of his own making, an exceedingly churchly volume, and soon afterwards, by way of contrast almost comic, as the legend of the Merrymount Press in a sketch of the Maypole round which Thomas Morton's godless crew was supposed to have danced. The *Optimum* was Updike's constant goal. His road to it was hard. The wayfarer was shy, under a cloak of aloofness, fastidious, sharp of tongue, exacting, but in all respects as critical of himself as of others—hardly an equipment that made for an easy march through life.

He was born in Providence in February 1860, of sound Rhode Island, Massachusetts, and, more remotely, Dutch, stock. An eighteenth-century Daniel Updike was on such terms with Dean Berkeley in his Rhode Island days that the future Bishop, on quitting America, gave him a silver flagon as a token of friendship. The flagon and the name of Berkeley were transmitted in due time to the Updike with whom we are now concerned. His father, by the way, was named Caesar Augustus—and who am I, a Mark Antony by descent, to think it strange? Our Rhode Island forbears must have had classical leanings.

Updike's backgrounds and beginnings would commonly be called advantages. But as an only child, with delicate health and a sensitive nature, he passed an unhappy boyhood, and when he was nearly eighteen years old experienced in the sudden death of his father a shock of more than passing effect. His mother, a woman of strong character and intelligence, was left to him, and until her death nearly twenty years later, they were inseparable and devoted companions. Yet he was conscious through life that a boy had better not be brought up by women only. In a recent summer, I am told, he looked with envy one day upon a number of young people at a seashore place disporting themselves in break-neck amusements, and contrasted their childhood with his own. Fears of everything, he said, were instilled into him. "Water," he went on, "was something that would drown you; fire would burn you, and dogs would bite you." My own remembrance of him in boyhood summers is that he took no part whatever in the tennis, sailing, and swimming in which his young contemporaries were finding pleasure. Nor did he ever present, except for a certain "filling-out" in his latest years, the figure of one to whom such exercises were natural. His physique and bearing, even the precision of his speech, were those of a man to whom the mind seemed more important than the body.

One may not, and would not, peep and botanize on the grave of a friend. When anybody makes so much of his life, however, as Updike did, the achievement shows only the more clearly if the handicaps and obstacles that precede it are frankly acknowledged. Besides those that have been mentioned, there was the plight of slender means, following his father's death. At a Providence private school, where the weekly declamations filled him with dread, he made his beginnings with books, and turned his taste for them to good account by serving for a time as an assistant in the Providence Athenaeum. This was another beginning — of a life-long intimacy with libraries. If he had gone, as he hoped, to college — Brown or Harvard—there is no reason to believe that he would have become ultimately more a scholar and civilized thinker than he was, for the college graduates who achieve precisely that are few. So are they who start, like Updike, at the bottom of a particular ladder and proceed to the top. The rung on which Updike first put his foot was that of an errand boy in the Boston publishing house of Houghton, Mifflin & Company. At twenty, as he was in 1880 when this work began, he was beyond the normal age for this rudimentary but trying post. Sticking to it through fatigues and discouragements, he was transferred from the business office of the firm in Boston to the Riverside Press in Cambridge, where his aptitude in matters of print began to count—also his taste, which was by no means confined to type.

Updike's earliest printed writings consisted of five unsigned articles in the "Contributors' Club" of the *Atlantic Monthly* in the years 1889 and 1890. They were little essays, with one exception relating entirely to observations in Europe. Many eminent writers have done worse in their twenties. One of these "Clubs" was devoted to a rendering into meritorious English verse, under the title *A French Folly*, of a long poem of François Coppée's on the Eiffel Tower. This was not only a token of Updike's self-cultivation, already well under way. Beyond that, and without reference to him, but of peculiar interest at this much later moment for its revelation of the seer in Coppée, are these stanzas written about the Tower in 1888: —

> *In revery on its highest plane,*
> *By sad presentiment I hear*
> *The German cannons' sullen roar*
> *Far eastward, on the French frontier.*
>
> *For on the day when France, in arms,*
> *Shall cast, with fatal throw, the die,*
> *With bitter tears shall we not look*
> *Where gold and iron wasted lie?*

The exceedingly churchly volume of which I have spoken was made under Updike's direction at the Riverside Press before he became a printer on his own account. It was a work of collaboration with his friend Harold Brown of Providence, who, besides sharing in Updike's ecclesiastical sympathies, could finance both this book, *On the Dedication of American Churches*, and the superb *Altar Book* which Updike published under the imprint of the Merrymount Press five years later, in 1896. The authors of the first appeared on its title-page merely as "Two Laymen of the Diocese of Rhode Island." Its dedication: "To the Right Reverend Father in God, Thomas, By Divine Permission Bishop of Rhode Island" was perhaps more strictly in the tradition of Anglican propriety than was the witty old Bishop Clark himself.

Like a number of young Bostonians of his earlier years,

Updike, according to his own statement, had little in common with American Protestantism. If the term Anglo-Catholicism had not yet come into common use, it was that to which he was devoted — and so sincerely that any sincerity less than his own annoyed or amused him. I remember the relish with which he related one experience of the time—at an early Easter service at the Cowley Fathers' Church of St. John the Evangelist. Passing through a vestibule door he found himself face to face with another young layman, who greeted him eagerly with "Christ is risen — give the proper answer!" Updike could give all the proper answers, but that was not the way to get them out of him. Equally foreign to him were the rather self-conscious activities of the young Jacobites, members of the "Order of the White Rose" who celebrated the Feast of Charles the Martyr with ceremonies of mourning and expiation and, for another outlet, tossed their "Pewter Mugs" and published their *Knight-Errant*. There are natural Bohemians, and there are those who outlive their Bohemianism. From this, in any of its forms, Updike was perpetually immune. Whatever partook of sham, in whatever degree, was anathema to him, and he was at no pains to conceal his scorn of it.

ALL this may seem a long preliminary to the story of the Merrymount Press. Perhaps it is justified by taking thought that Updike's work was so much an expression of his personality that the one can hardly be understood without some knowledge of the other. Pretence and compromise were equally foreign to his nature. This was as true of his printing as of everything else about him.

When, still at Riverside with no sufficient prospect of advancement, he made up his mind to become a better all-round printer than was commonly thought worth while, he knew that this end could be attained only in an establishment of his own. As he looked back after forty years on the beginnings of his business in two rooms on an upper story of an old house at the corner of Beacon Street and Tremont Place in Boston, he could not wonder that the valor he displayed was regarded as ignorance. "I required capital," he wrote, "and had little; comprehension of my own trade, of which I had less; and business experience, of which I had none at all." He did not permit himself any illusions about his work, either when he undertook it or afterwards. Thus he referred to it all in a bit of autobiography which he contributed in 1930 to a Boy Scouts' pamphlet on Printing: "There is one encouraging thing to be learned from what I have done — that starting with no education, not much health, little money, and a generally poor and unpractical training for life, and being pushed by necessity into printing, a work that I hated, by studying that work and persistently keeping at it, I have succeeded in it better than some men, and, in spite of many handicaps, made myself over, through it."

To these words he added others, of which the following set forth a philosophy of life and work, not for printers only: "What we specially need in these United States is an intensive cultivation of the field that is given a man to till — not talking about it, or writing about it, but working at it. If you do this, by and by, after years of effort, success and failure, you will become so good at your work, that you will be (just as I am) asked to tell how you did it! — which appears to be the lowest rung on the ladder of Fame!"

It was certainly a happy thought to name his enterprise the Merrymount Press. Established in 1893, it was not definitely so called until three years later, and while it still needed to be made known, he declared the Maypole of Merrymount "a symbol of happiness found in workaday things; of a high aim and pleasure in trying to attain it, an ideal to which the Merry-mount Press has endeavored to be true." Many details of its attainment are set forth in Updike's own *Notes* already quoted. Here it would be superfluous to follow them at all minutely — the migrations from smaller to constantly larger quarters, always harmonized in taste, through old furniture and prints, with the work proceeding from the Press; the relations between management and "help"; the fortunate association with Mr. John Bianchi, foreman until he became partner in 1915. Through the hands of Updike and Bianchi, under whom the business is now continued, it has been estimated that some twenty thousand pieces of printing have passed during the first forty years of the Press. The rule that nothing was too small or trivial for close personal supervision has accounted for much. Under the further principle of Merrymount that it should remain a small establishment, the number of employees has seldom exceeded thirty.

Updike's equipment for the adventure of the Press has been excellently defined by Mr. W. A. Dwiggins as "an aesthetic predilection, a philosophy of life, and friends." These elements have already been suggested. The technical aspects of Updike's work may be left to printers and designers, writing as specialists for special readers. The experts will assign him to his particular place, among the loftiest, in the hierarchy of printers, relating him duly to past and present masters of the craft. In more general terms it is to be said that friends at the start are a blessing in every endeavor, and also that they are of no avail unless the befriended proves worthy of their belief in him. This is precisely what Updike did with the *Altar Book* which he could not have undertaken but for his friend Harold Brown. His philosophy of life was a religious philosophy, taking its outward form in the Anglican Church, for he was a traditionalist as well as a perfectionist. Thus he brought to the making of a book designed for clerical use in the service of Holy Communion a complete understanding and sympathy. His aesthetic sense led him to choose, from his young contemporaries in Boston, the supremely gifted Bertram Grosvenor Goodhue as the designer of borders, initials, and special type. For a few full-page illustrations he turned to England and enlisted the services of Robert Anning Bell — also of Sir John Stainer for bits of musical notation. In the early nineties, when this book was in preparation, William Morris and his Kelmscott Press were having their effect upon what was called the Renaissance of American printing. The influence was noticeable in Updike's *Altar Book*, but only to a limited extent, and it did not continue. The standards of a cool lucidity, closely related to the rules of common-sense, were fundamental in Updike; he called for legibility as the first requisite of anything meant to be read. On these standards he proceeded to build, freed, again by common-sense quickened by imagination, from any fetish of the superiority of work by hand, and demonstrating beyond doubt that the most modern labor-saving mechanisms of the printer's trade could be employed under intelligent direction, with the best of results.

Of these results in general Updike himself wrote: "I have been classed by my work as a conservative, but I am a liberal conservative or a conservative liberal — whichever you like or dislike. All I wish to conserve, either in traditionalism or modernism, is common sense." In another place he suggested the relation of his whole life to his printing: "One is automatically either a critic or an enthusiast of modern trends in literature, music, art, and daily living, so we unconsciously govern our printing by the kind of life we approve." With him it was the life and the printing of a liberal conservative.

The mention of Goodhue and other helpers in the production of the *Altar Book* suggests what became a continuing alertness of Updike's — to recognize ability even in beginners, and to employ it for the Merrymount Press. The names of W. A. Dwiggins and T. M. Cleland, now well known, were relatively unfamiliar when Updike first printed their designs; and of Rudolph Ruzicka — both designer and friend — it is enough to say that from 1912 till 1941, excepting only the year 1925, he was the producer of the cherished "Annual Keepsakes, Printed for the Friends of the Merrymount Press." These twenty-nine wood engravings, in color, of views in and about Boston, the beauty of each enlivened by a Latin text of singular aptness chosen by Updike himself, can hardly fail to become collector's items treasured for the sheer pleasure of possessing them.

Among the friends who helped him both by counsel and by patronage in the earlier days of the Press was Charles Eliot Norton, about to quit the scene as a guide and arbiter of

American taste. Another was Edith Wharton, who required of the Scribners, on publishing her first volume of short stories, that it should be printed at the Merrymount Press. This was not quite the first, or by any means the last, of the trade books manufactured by Updike for publishers in New York and Boston. Privately-printed books — family chronicles and the like, — year-books for churches, annual reports, school and college catalogues, club publications, programs, all the varieties of job-work which a printing-house is glad to undertake, issued year after year in growing volume from the Merrymount Press. Happily there was no quarrel with Dr. Holmes' principle of "small fevers thankfully received." If the work was regarded as expensive, it is only to be remembered that a large number of discriminating patrons found it worth while to meet the cost attaching to the productions of highly-qualified specialists who spared no pains to give of their meticulous best. Not every printing-house is thoughtful enough in making a program for a musicale in a private house to use paper so soft that no rustling is audible; or to check up a European journey of 1833 by means of road-maps and guide-books of the time; or in printing *Benjamin Franklin on Balloons*, with a Montgolfier balloon on the title-page, to secure from a French paper-making Montgolfier of the present, descended from the aeronaut, a specially-made paper with a balloon watermark.

The standard *Book of Common Prayer of the Protestant Episcopal Church* is regarded as the acme of Updike's work. All his liturgical learning and typographical skill were brought to bear upon the production of the folio volume, of the highest dignity and beauty, from which all the Prayer Books printed since its completion in 1930 are page-for-page copies, with uniform pagination whatever their size.

THERE are fugitive writings and several small books on which Updike's right to the title of scholar might well be based. There is, however, one work, his monumental *Printing Types*

in two volumes, which gives him a place among the really
learned. It had its origin in a course of lectures at the Harvard
School of Business Administration. A searching study of
types at home and in European travel, and first-hand intimacy with their use, qualified him to speak with a rare
authority. The extensive re-writing, and the choice and explanation of numberless illustrations before the book could
be published in 1922, were labors of genuine erudition. Second
and third printings were called for in 1923 and 1927, and in
1937 a revised and enlarged edition met the continued demand
for the book which has come to be called — by others, be it
noted, than Updike himself — "The Printers' Bible."

Printing Types won for its author the honorary degree of
Master of Arts at Harvard in 1929, even as the re-issue in 1907
of *The History of the Narrangansett Church* by his grandfather, Wilkins Updike, gave to Brown University the occasion to honor him with the same degree, which the grandfather
had received on the appearance of the same book in its original
form in 1847. Updike was wont to deplore his lack of a formal
education: in fact he was a shining illustration of the familiar
truth that self-education often produces the best results of all.

The trouble with many scholars is that they lack precisely
the cultivation, the sense of proportion between their own
interests and those of the larger world of general urbanity,
which Updike possessed, to the constant and increasing advantage of his writing. He could draw at will, for instance,
upon an abundant store of apt quotation, for which he took
no credit, saying that his mind was equipped with a number
of little drawers, which would pop out with needed words
at the call of a retentive memory. Both his talk and his writing
were quickened by this gift, which indeed was only one of
the elements that gave to the best of his writing a positive
distinction and charm. Witness, besides the books already
mentioned, the papers collected in the two small volumes, *In
the Day's Work*, and the last of his publications, *Some Aspects
of Printing Old and New*. There is also his *Richard Smith,
First English Settler of the Narragansett Country, Rhode*

Island, dealing, after the best fashion of the pious antiquarian, with progenitors of his own.

As a man of the world he was not, to be sure, of the sort that suffers fools at all gladly, but he impaled them with his wit less frequently in his printed writings than in his talk and correspondence. In these he often seemed to echo the Silver Swan in the song of Orlando Gibbons — "More geese than swans now live, more fools than wise." He chose his diversions and companions with much care, discarding readily those that were not for him. He used to tell a story of a child who was held up before a window to see a passing procession, and soon complained, "My buttons hurt more than I can see." In terms of adult choice, Updike was just as sure of his own preferences.

That sense of the fitness of things to which I have alluded developed early in him, together with a humorous recognition of its opposite. Late in his life he recalled the first Washington's Birthday party he attended, with a special remembrance of a head of George Washington in vanilla ice-cream, mated, not with Martha, but with a strawberry ice-cream rabbit — "the last emblem applicable to a childless pair."

To the loneliness of his later years it is hard to believe that he would not have preferred a family life of his own and the perpetuation of a name of which he was naturally proud. If he never married, it was not because he shared at all in the confirmed celibate's scorn of matrimony. In its place he made the most of his friendships, whether, through these later years, in the house he occupied in Boston, or at his farm in Vermont, far from his associations with Lenox and Newport. In the beauty and peace of the country-side, in the simplicity of his surroundings, innocent of the cares of business, his sense of reality found a satisfaction of which both the visitors who came to share it and the devoted Italian couple who ministered to him for many years were keenly aware. Younger fellow-craftsmen were among the friends to whom he gave himself with least reserve; and so, early and late, were intelligent, witty, and sympathetic women, with whom a feminine quality of sensitiveness in his own perceptions gave him a special kinship of spirit. There was something of the older world about him and—Yankee as he was—something Gallic, something consequently in the essence of his mind and wit that made him turn, as cultivated French Abbés of the eighteenth century turned, to the society of congenial women. Of course there were Abbés and Abbés, but if one only knew the life and letters of pre-Revolutionary France as well as he did, it would be possible to name the very Abbé to whom he might be likened with some accuracy. With respect to less intimate human relations, it was like him to observe that a man who came to see him on a matter of business expected to encounter a mixture of King Solomon in wisdom and a wild-cat in manners, and was surprised to find a normal human being. Such a creature as this visitor expected to meet would never have indulged himself in little plays of wit which Updike enjoyed— such, for example, as the Wordsworthian lines "On a Wash-Cloth Left on a Visit to the Lake Country by the Printer Rogers," received by Bruce Rogers after a country visit to Updike.

Distressed as he was by tendencies of the times quite out of keeping with standards he set for himself and by the signs of chaos in world affairs, he found a countervailing comfort in the recognition of his labors by those best qualified to pass upon them. Year after year since the American Institute of Graphic Arts began its annual exhibitions of "Fifty Books of the Year" in 1923, the productions of the Merrymount Press have received signal honors. In 1940 the Institute and the Grolier Club joined in arranging a display of the work of Updike and his Press in the exhibition room of the Club, and marked the occasion by publishing a pamphlet with the addresses made by Royal Cortissoz and others, with Updike's response, and an admirable check-list of the books, pamphlets, and articles written and edited by Updike. Since his death, the Huntington Library has prepared an exhibition commemorated in a pamphlet, *The Work of the Merrymount Press and Its Founder, Daniel Berkeley Updike* (1860-1941).

Stretching thus across our continent, his fame has long been established also beyond these boundaries. His labors may truly be said to have had a world-wide reward.

IN THE bit of autobiography which Updike wrote for the Boy Scouts' manual he said: "I became a printer by accident. If I have become a good printer — not more — it is through intention and determination, and the intention has got hold of me to such an extent that printing has become to me — with one exception — the most interesting thing in the world." For those who knew him there can be little doubt that this one exception was the church, religion, God, and the soul of man — however you may choose to define a sphere of life and thought which was paramount with him, as it was with the best of Abbés. May not the pursuing of a trade in the spirit of a profession be merely the regarding of one's job as a vocation in the sense of a commission from higher powers?

Order is heaven's first law — and it was Updike's. I have already spoken of him as a traditionalist. In the church of his forefathers for several centuries, and of his own upbringing, he found an order, an authority, which met his own deep sense of tradition and of human need. "It seems," he once wrote a friend, "as if religion and God as found in it, is the only thing in the world that understands because it knows the whole story. It is the great Friend, who knows our troubles and deficiencies without being told: and one sometimes meets something like that in people, though only rarely." For another friend he copied from a notebook of his own this fragment of Richard Bentley's translation of Manilius: "Wherefore see we the stars arise in their season, and move as at a word spoken, on the paths appointed for them? Of whom there is none that hastens, neither is there any that tarries behind. Why are the summer nights beautiful with these that change not, and the nights of winter from of old? These things are not the work of chance, but the order of a God most high."

With this sense of the nearness of God, it was natural for Updike, on successive Eves of All Saints' Day, to light the candles on each side of a Madonna and Child on the press-room side of a door to his office, and to observe the Day himself in worship and remembrance. To faith, however, he added works, and of a sort which could not have been easy for him. This, for a number of years, was the regular visiting of inmates of the State Prison at Charlestown, and befriending them on their release. There was an instance of taking one of these men into his own employ, after telling the man's story to those who were to work beside him, and ensuring his welcome. The church, for Updike, was by no means all of Christianity. His outward devotion to it took many forms, including expressions of loyalty to his own past in the shape of memorials in the Rhode Island South County churches with which his ancestors were associated. Here, too, there was a secular loyalty, prompting gifts to a local school, library, and hospital.

Have we strayed too far from the printer? I think not, and for a reason that will stand repeating — that the work and the personality of Updike were immitigably bound together. If the work is an object of interest outside his immediate circle, the personality, surrounded in that circle with personal reserves, must also be regarded. The two were very much of a piece. For his life and for his art — which he preferred to call his trade — there was a single standard. This can be shown hardly better than in a passage of his own carefully considered writing on the final pages of his *Printing Types:*—

For the printer there are two camps, and only two, to be in: one, the camp of things as they are; the other, that of things as they should be. The first camp is on a level and extensive plain, and many eminently respectable persons lead lives of comfort therein; the sport is, however, inferior! The other camp is more interesting. Though on an inconvenient hill, it commands a wide view of typography, and in it are the class that help on sound taste in printing, because they are willing to make sacrifices for it. This group is small, accomplishes little comparatively, but has the one saving grace of honest endeavor — *it tries*. Like Religion, "it will remain a voice crying in the wilderness; but it will believe what it cries, and there will be some to listen to it in the future, as there have been many in the past." Around this camp idealistic lunatics hover, but they are quite harmless, and were never known to hurt or print anything seriously. This camp I think the only one worth living in. You may not make all the money you want, but will have all you need, and you will have a tremendously good time, for as Stevenson said, "work that we really love is nothing more than serious play."

With these words of his, rather than any of my own, Updike, the printer and the human being, may be left in the camp of things as they should be.

THE MERRYMOUNT PRESS
OF BOSTON

GEORGE PARKER WINSHIP

T HE MERRYMOUNT PRESS is a commercial establishment
at Boston, Massachusetts, belonging to Daniel Berkeley
Updike, who founded it in 1893, and to his partner John
Bianchi. It has a reputation for doing work of unexceptional
excellence. Mr. Updike was born in the neighboring state of
Rhode Island, of an old and well-connected family, and he
inherited decided preferences for things of high quality.
When he completed his elementary schooling, it was necessary for him to earn his own living, and a relative secured him
a position with the publishing house of Houghton, Mifflin &
Company of Boston. This firm was maintaining a recognized
prestige as the publishers of the *Atlantic Monthly* magazine
and of the authors who had written the most esteemed works
of American literature. Updike remained in their office for
ten years and as he showed an interest in the way things were
printed, the details of getting out the firm's advertising were
turned over to him. A certain amount of minor book-work
likewise fell into his hands. He had his own ideas of how things
ought to look when they were finished, and as the firm was
prosperous he was able occasionally to induce the printers to
make changes until he secured results that pleased him. It was
a slow, and expensive, method of self-education, which led
him in time to perceive that he could do his work better if he
knew more about the operation of a printing-shop. The Riverside Press, at which the Houghton Mifflin books are made,
belonged to members of that firm, so he arranged to be transferred to the Press, where for two years he worked at the
routine of actual book-making.

At this time the "Revival of Printing" was in full bloom. It
was an offshoot of the Arts-and-Crafts movement of the 1880's,

which had been transplanted by William Morris, who had energized it into an exotic luxuriance. The cultured classes everywhere, and the larger number of persons who aspired to be regarded as cultured, were attracted by the glowing splendor of Morris' Kelmscott publications. The patronage of fine printing came to be widely recognized as the surest way to affiliate oneself with the intellectual aristocracy. As the Kelmscott books were also rapidly increasing in money value, this created an active demand for all sorts of other publications which were privately-printed or were put out with the appearance of typographical excellence. The "Revival" did its best to kill itself by over-excitation, but it proved to have sturdy roots strong enough to withstand the strain of the spectacular fungi. The spirit within the Arts-and-Crafts movement had developed a healthy appreciation of things that are fundamentally well-made, as well as attractive to live with. When the time came, this appreciation of good, every-day things asserted its right to have what it wanted, including well-made books.

Updike saw a good deal of this movement, and became convinced that it was making a permanent impression upon the American community. He likewise came to the conclusion that he wanted to make books for a living, but he saw clearly that his ideas about how to do this could only be carried out if he were absolutely unhampered. It is typical of him that his idea of being his own master included independence of customers as well as of colleagues or collaborators. His employers, when he told them of his intentions, realized the importance of what he had been doing for them and offered him an attractive opportunity to remain on their staff. But as his mind was made up to go ahead by himself, after a while they found someone else, a young Westerner named Bruce Rogers.

A circular letter "To the Trade," copyrighted in 1893, inaugurated the new venture. The date, and the venturer's later achievements, give this document considerable historical significance. Its appearance as well as much of its contents need to be interpreted in the light of the "Revival of Printing" and of William Morris' Kelmscott Press. From the "Revival" as a conscious movement, Updike held himself aloof after he began his independent career, and it appears to have influenced him almost none at all. He watched it closely and experimented with some of its formulae, as anyone with his opportunities and his intellectual and professional curiosity was bound to do, but there is no sign of his being warped from his own individual course. The main portion of this first circular is a statement of his purpose and aims. Its significance lies in the fact that the following extracts are as true of the Merrymount Press later as they were when written in 1893:

"He is now prepared to undertake for such of the trade as desire it...decorative printing and book-making. Typography and design in its relation thereto have long been Mr. Updike's special study, and he has also a practical knowledge of the commercial necessities of the work in which he is engaged . . . Illustrations or decorations will be designed under his direction, or he will advise as to the persons best fitted to make them.

"The style of typography will be [the tense of the verb should be noted] set by him. He endeavors to keep himself informed about the best English, French and American work [he would not now repeat the rest of the sentence] that he may be enabled to give books those touches which are nowadays necessary if a volume is to be a success.

"Limited editions of attractive little books of poems or essays printed on hand-made paper, with initials and bordered title-pages [delete: in the modern aesthetic English style] he makes a specialty.

"Every publisher and book-seller is called upon to undertake an occasional privately-printed or commission book, which, while it often has little commercial value, takes up a great deal of time and gives much trouble. Persons having such books to print, and desiring well-appointed volumes in small editions, may be referred direct to Mr. Updike.

"The above applies to genealogies and family and local histories, which are often the work of amateurs. Clear, practical arrangement is of the first importance here, and they should also be good pieces of bookmaking. Reports of clubs, institutions, charities, libraries, etc., will be well printed in appropriate style . . . Pamphlets, circulars, catalogues, etc., intended for advertising purposes will also be prepared, for there is no class of printing to which more care and thought may be given than attractive advertising.

"Service-Books, Books of Devotion, Memorial Sermons and Addresses, services for Christmas, Easter, etc., and all other forms of ecclesiastical printing of a rich yet simple sort, in accordance with the best traditions of such work, will be gladly undertaken."

Thirty-five years later, this statement of a program leaves the historian of the Merrymount Press nothing to say, except that this is what Mr. Updike is still doing successfully. He has done all the kinds of work that he said he wanted to do, and comparatively little else. Implied in the circular, but not stated explicitly for obvious reasons, is the intimation that he was going to do each piece of work as he thought it ought to be done. It is this determination, persistently adhered to, which has given the Press its fame and its commercial success.

Before he began work on his own account, Updike had made one book, and only one, in which he had had entirely his own way. It is a simple volume, with little that is distinctive or decorative about it, except that there is nothing wrong; the proportions of page and margins, title, size of types and composition, tone of paper, and quality of press-work offer nothing for obvious criticism. The book is *An Inquiry into the Naming of Churches in the United States,* compiled by two laymen of the Diocese of Rhode Island, that is, Mr. Updike and his closest friend, Harold Brown of Newport. The two had grown up together and were bound by common tastes and prejudices, but chiefly by a strong attachment to the ritual of their church. Their friendship had an important influence upon the Merrymount Press. Every successful printer aspires sooner or later to produce a monumental volume which shall embody all his typographical ideals. Ordinarily this is undertaken toward the close of a prosperous career, and in not a few instances it has brought that career to an unhappy end, for elaborate large volumes are costly to produce and they rarely sell satisfactorily. It was Updike's particular good fortune to do what is still his most pretentious volume first of all, and to do it so well that he has not had any uncontrollable desire to make another essay in that direction. This was the *Altar Book*, which was announced in his first circular and which holds an assured place as "typographically and decoratively the best piece of Church work yet produced." The quoted characterization was the printer's expressed hope before the plans were consummated. The finished work may have fallen short of his ideals then, just as it fails to satisfy his matured taste, but it pleased those for whom it was designed, then and now, and it still maintains a primacy among liturgical publications.

The *Altar Book* was made possible by the friend with whom he had compiled the nomenclature of the American churches. Mr. Brown shared the printer's idealism in the fullest measure, and his standards of the highest excellence did not recognize the necessity for any qualification or limitation. His financial generosity enabled Mr. Updike to state in a later announcement that: "It has been undertaken without desire to hamper it either in the expenditure of time or money, and it is believed that the elimination of these two factors has enabled the publisher to produce a volume which shall be of lasting value."

Time was not so important during the first two years of the venture, but the command of money made it easier to get what was wanted, without undue delays, from those upon whom he was dependent for an outstanding excellence. The type-setting and press-work were done under his immediate oversight and to his satisfaction, but the permanent reputation of the volume, as a monument of ecclesiastical book-making, is due even more to the fact that he went to Sir John Stainer for precisely the right music; to Robert Anning Bell for the full-page drawings which rank with the finest that have ever added to the spirit of a devotional work; to Bertram Grosvenor Goodhue for the decorative borders and the initial letters embodying the correct symbolism or suggestiveness for each page or paragraph with which they are used; and to Charles Sherborn for the engraving of the armorial colophon design.

The *Altar Book* came out in the spring of 1896. This was when the Kelmscott Chaucer was on the press, approaching completion, and the stories of its matchless beauties had aroused wide public interest. Every magazine reader knew that printing had been revived, that William Morris had done it, and that fine printing meant what Morris was doing. When Updike wrote in 1893 of "those touches which are nowadays necessary if a volume is to be a success," he meant borders and initials in the Kelmscott manner and heavy black type such as Morris liked. The *Altar Book* conformed to these unquestioned standards of its day. Equally in his circulars and in such of the work of those years as has been seen, there is the same acceptance of Morris' dominating influence.

Nevertheless, there is a significant difference between the work turned out by the designers employed by Updike, and that of the greater artist whose leadership they acknowledged by their imitation of him. Looking back from a generation later, it is possible to perceive that Morris came to his great undertaking of the Kelmscott Press with his vitality waning, and that his designs for the borders and initials, magnificent as they are, lack the variety and the freshness of imagination which pervade his cretonnes and his wall-papers and other earlier achievements. No one else could approach him in technical skill or in decorative instinct. It is none the less true that Updike got his designers to do just what Morris ought to have been doing. They did things in the Kelmscott manner, but they were working for a man who insisted upon appropriateness, originality of conception, and carefulness in execution, quite beyond that of anybody else at that time.

Goodhue had the American field largely to himself for decorative work of first-rate quality. But his architectural work was already demanding all his best efforts, and it became necessary for the printer to find substitutes who could execute the commissions that were coming in steadily-increasing numbers. For this purpose he established relations with the Birmingham Guild of Handicraft, and for the next few years Miss Mary Newill and others of the Guild supplied him with some very charming designs. He became their American representative and the agent for their organ, *The Quest*, until it passed away along the route strewn with the wrecks of amateur idealism. The circular in which he notified his correspondents that *The Quest* was to be discontinued, is of interest on account of his evident annoyance caused by the unbusinesslike habits of these talented English friends. From the very beginning, Updike had clearly recognized that the chief danger he faced was the reputation for dilettantism, with all that this implied in popular estimation. His announcements repeatedly stressed the fact that he was in business as a regular, ordinary printer, ready and willing to execute any sort of work that came his way — provided that he could do it in what he thought was the best way.

Mr. Updike's primary interest was the designing and making of books, but for a time it looked as if he would be obliged to become a publisher as well, in order to keep busy. The *Altar Book* sold better than had been expected, and was followed by other ventures, so that he was able to issue a regular list of his own publications. The first two were *Vexilla Regis*, a devotional year-book, and Hans Christian Andersen's *The Nightingale*. A new translation of *Don Quixote by* George Santayana was announced, but through no fault of the printer this never went to press. Its place on the list was taken by an edition of the *Agricola* and other minor works of Tacitus, edited by Professor Morris H. Morgan of Harvard, which was finished in 1904.

The Tacitus was in effect a belated reply to Morris' dictum that there had been no good printing since the fifteenth century. This had come to be a shibboleth of the Revivalists. As his comment on it, Updike selected a text which had been printed in the fifteenth century and printed it in the fifteenth-century manner, better than any fifteenth-century book was done. It is a short text, forty pages, so that the perfection of its press-work, the uniformity of color, the unvarying correctness of every detail, do not become monotonous. In spite of all these virtues, and because of them, the Tacitus does not satisfy the ordinary person's aesthetic feeling in the way the older books do. The reason is simple, although it was not perceived until after another quarter-century of active attention to fine book-making. The earliest books are satisfying, because they are not perfect. There is something about the slight unevenness of inking and the variations in the paper which give a human quality that the perfect machining of modern work never gets. No more does it come from the artificiality of hand press-work under present-day conditions. The Kelmscott and Doves Press books, made by hand, have less of this charm than the Vale and Merrymount volumes which were machined on presses that embody every device of the mechanical experts. The problem that now confronts the makers of fine books is how to regain this human quality without affectation and without absurdity. The problem is not insoluble, but the solution is not yet in sight.

The *Altar Book*, in accordance with the dictates of the time, was set in a new type designed especially for it. Morris had declared that no good type was purchasable, and moreover every fifteenth-century printer began work with a new type-face designed for his individual use. Consequently each up-to-date private press of the 'nineties began by securing a new type not like any other. That of the *Altar Book* is on the whole admirable, and it shows even better in the Tacitus than in the book for which it was cut. It is described in a circular dated October 15, 1894, as "A Great Primer type which, while entirely clear to the eye, has great richness, solidity, and blackness." When the taste of book-lovers swings back to the gothic, as it is sure to do some day, this type is certain to come into its own as marking a high point in typographic evolution. With the reaction from decoration which followed the death of Morris, however, it went into oblivion.

A perfect new type face is the *ignis fatuus* of every printer who dreams of reaching the slopes of Olympus. Jenson caught it once, and Caslon domesticated it, but it has eluded all the others. Updike made his cast at it when he commissioned Herbert P. Horne to design a face which was christened Mont-allegro after the Press. It is very good indeed, but like the later, and perhaps better, face which the same designer produced for Philip Lee Warner's Medici Society, it has everything that a perfect type should have, except complete adaptability to the human eye. The designer had stipulated that he should have the first use of the Montallegro type for a new translation by himself of Condivi's life of Michelangelo, to be produced in accordance with his own specifications. This explains why this book is unlike anything else with the Merrymount imprint. The type shows to much better advantage in the volume of *The Humanists' Library*, into which Updike put more of himself than into anything else that carries his name.

Humanism means the Renaissance, which in turn is the background of the roman type upon which good bookmaking is dependent. When the Revival shook itself free from the medieval dicta of Morris and accepted the idea that no book can claim to be good unless it is easily read by ordinary people, the roman type resumed its dominant position. Updike welcomed this return to normal, and sought an opportunity to point the way along what he believed to be the right road. With the enthusiastic approval of Charles Eliot Norton and other advisers who felt that a new cultural era was dawning, he announced that he would print a series of books which might be considered as the gospel of this twentieth-century re-awakening. Pierre de Nolhac's *Petrarch*, Sidney's *Defence of Poesie*, Leonardo on Art and Life, and *Erasmus Against War*, were issued in 1906-1908 to show the scope of the plan. A list of twenty-four additional titles was printed, from which subscribers were asked to select their preferences, as a guide in deciding upon further issues. The price of the first series was $6.00 each. This was reduced to $3.00 when two volumes of a second series were issued in 1913, so that nothing might stand in the way of a wide public distribution. The change in price probably settled the fate of the undertaking, for although the volumes of the second series are typographically much better than those of the first, many who would have supported a costly and exclusive offering, lost interest in the attempt to place books like these within reach of the many. The number of copies was not limited in the usual meaning of that term, but no more were printed than could be sold, so that they soon went out of print. Nothing was left out of any of these volumes that Updike knew how to put into them in order to make them satisfy his humanistic ideals, and those who possess the series have one of the significant land-marks of modern typography.

As he now had work enough to do, for other people, to keep himself and his employees busy, he gave up further ideas of Merrymount Press publications. For his own gratification, he issued from the Press two books about the section of his native state with which his family had been identified. These were a new edition of *A History of the Narragansett Church* by Wilkins Updike, and the Diary of the Reverend James MacSparran, the first Church of England clergyman settled on the western shores of Narrangansett Bay. With these two ought to be associated a group of books privately-printed for various members of the Hazard family, all of which deal with this same Narragansett country. There is no other twenty-five square miles in the United States, and probably not elsewhere, whose traditions have been preserved in so distinguished a group of printed volumes.

While the *Altar Book* was in hand, the printer realized that its type would not serve his purpose if he were to succeed in getting commissions from regular publishers. He needed something that was not noticeably different from the usual type-faces, but which would at the same time enable him to assure his customers that it was out of the ordinary. Therefore, when he went to England to perfect the arrangements for the *Altar Book*, he sought for unusual faces which seemed to him good but which had passed out of current use. He extended this search to the Continent when he took another holiday after the *Altar Book* was off his mind. Upon his return from this trip, he moved to larger quarters around the corner from his first office at No. 6 Beacon Street, and announced the transfer to No. 7 Tremont Place in a circular "To the Trade . . . Some Notes on new Types, Papers, and Wood Blocks, lately collected in France, England, and Italy."

"During his recent journey abroad Mr. Updike enlarged his present interesting fonts of old-style types, to such proportions that he is now equipped for book-work.

"Among founts new to the Merrymount Press are several interesting series of English types dating from the beginning of this [nineteenth] century, with their appropriate ornaments; a series of French types after the best old models; a series of Roman types of the sixteenth century from the original matrices; and some Dutch and Italian series of figures and initials.

"Some old Italian wood-blocks and French copper-plates, a stock of old hand-made paper from a mill in the north of Italy, and marbled paper of the eighteenth century, have also been bought."

This is commonplace, thirty years later, when these things have come to be the stock in trade of every private printer and fancy book-maker, but in 1896 it was something that had not been done before. Shortly after this he secured some fonts of Scotch modern face. It was used for the novels of Edith Wharton, printed for Charles Scribner's Sons, and has ever since held a favored place with him for books designed for general circulation.

A circular dated 1898 announced the addition of a font of Spanish Italic, and added that "The work of the Press has more than doubled even during the past year. . . . A new press specially constructed for very delicate work has also been installed."

This new press was of some historical significance, for it was purchased just at the time when an English disciple of

Morris proclaimed that he was the legitimate successor to the Master, because he had secured the actual hand-presses upon which the Kelmscott books had been printed, and that he would continue to produce books printed on them by the very same hands. Perhaps Updike's most important single contribution toward assuring the permanence of the Arts-and-Crafts movement was his puncturing of the "hand-work" fetish, so far as printing is concerned. He demonstrated, and has continued to prove, that there is no harm in the machine so long as the man who operates it maintains his control of it, and of himself, instead of being controlled by it. The Merrymount Press has added to its equipment the most modern of machines, capable of turning off very good work at a high rate of speed. But these machines are never permitted to show what they might do, because they do better work at a moderate rate, with ink that is not adapted to high speed. The best is none too good for the Merrymount Press, in every detail of its equipment, but it must serve to produce the best, and not be served by the usual competitive requirements.

By profession, Mr. Updike is a successful business man, attending diligently to the demands of an enterprise which is, even more than most, dependent upon his individual oversight of details. His Press is in many ways the expression of his personality. It is equally true that his private life has always gone on independently of his business, and no small part of his success is due to the impersonal attitude which he has scrupulously maintained toward its management and its output. One of the rare exceptions to this was when he chose the name for his Press. A High Church Episcopalian from a state that still glories in the fact that it was founded by men who were not allowed to live in Massachusetts, Updike had gone to Boston to set himself up in business. He thereupon chose as his emblem the Maypole of Merrymount, a seventeenth-century settlement midway between the Puritans of Boston and the Pilgrims of Plymouth. At Merrymount the original settler, another Church of England man named Thomas Morton, had tried to inject gaiety into those neighbors. Of him our printer wrote: "This joyous Englishman believed that labor is none the worse for having a little pleasure mingled with its daily round; and it is hoped that the product of the Press will show the good results of work undertaken in somewhat the same spirit."

Judged by its fruits, it has been a somewhat sedate joyousness. This may help to explain why Mr. Updike has remained in Boston as a highly esteemed citizen, whereas Thomas Morton was soon driven out of the community he had thought of enlivening.

The Maypole and the name Merrymount are also reminiscent of much that was said at Arts-and-Crafts gatherings in those days. Morris interpreted this talk about the joyousness of labor in terms of the thirteenth century. It is characteristic of Updike that he found the same thing independently in the nineteenth. As his business prospered, less was said about the conditions under which it was carried on. The time that might have gone into talk was spent in considering ways of making the worker's lot pleasanter and more profitable for all concerned. The Merrymount crew of 1898, and of 1928, are not known to drop their work in order to gambol about the Maypole or the tea cups, but they seem to be even more contented with their lot than were the Merrymounters of three centuries ago.

Many of the employees appear to share with the owner a disinclination toward any change that disturbs the routine of the establishment. A part of the success of the Press has been due to the good fortune which provided it with its first workman, John Bianchi, a native of Renazzo in northern Italy. The work proved to be the kind he liked, and the standards upon which his employer insisted were those which he set for himself. The two men came to see and to think very much alike, without losing independence of judgment or the mutual confidence bred of strong character and occasional differences of opinion. As the work and the force of workers grew, Bianchi maintained his position at their head, doing everything as need arose in a way to satisfy himself, a severer critic than the owner. More and more responsibility rested with him, so that it was hardly more than the formalizing of what had come to be their relationship when in 1915 Mr. Updike announced that Mr. Bianchi had become his partner.

In somewhat the same mood that had dictated the choice of a name for the Press, Updike removed it after a few months from the mercantile building on Tremont Place to the street floor of a charming old residence at 104 Chestnut Street, between Beacon Hill and the Charles River. This was then a shabby-genteel neighborhood, frequented by artists and handi-crafters who were holding out against the inroads of slummier conditions. It seemed to be an ideal location for the youthful Press. The owner lived on the second story, whither he retired with favored clients for tea and toast at a proper time. Everything was exactly as it should be, for a story-book. In practice, it did not work well in the closing years of the nineteenth century. Customers came, bringing their friends, and the friends' friends followed, not always bringing business but invariably toward tea time. Everybody was most enthusiastic about everything, but the visitors found it hard to believe that real work was being done, for real money, under such idealistic conditions. None the less, the business kept on expanding until it reached the point where it seemed wise to install presses large enough to handle the work more economically. The floors of the old house would not stand their weight, and in consequence the Press was moved in 1903 to different quarters at 232 Summer Street, Boston. It occupies the top story of an office building, conveniently located directly across from the principal railway station of the city. The change gave the workers light and air, and what was important for the Arts-and-Crafts movement, a chance to show how the rooms of such a building could be made habitable and pleasant to work in, without detracting from the utilitarian advantages.

Since its establishment on Summer Street, the story of the Press is told chiefly by the bibliography of its output. And once more, the results are best described by the statement of the founder's intention. In 1898 he wrote that "his aim is to vary his work so widely that the distinguishing mark of the Press will not be a certain 'manner' but an excellence in many manners," or, as repeated a few months later, "an excellence in whatever manner is most suitable to the work intrusted to his care."

The Press has at times seemed on the verge of establishing its mannerisms. For a while the pages were set higher on the paper than before or since. There was a period when it caught the virus of close spacing. Paragraph indentations disappeared for a short time. The efforts to find out where the page numbers should go, do not count, for this is the puzzle no printer has solved. But like the earlier Morris influence, each tendency was thrown off before it became a fixed habit. Long before English contemporaries settled their minds upon readableness as the one and only test of good book-making, the Merrymount had adopted this as its working practice. It has held fast to this rule ever since. Except where some special reason exists for ornamentation, a Merrymount book is one that can be read from beginning to end without distraction.

This rule inevitably makes for severity. Not everyone wants to read the books he buys, and there has been criticism of Updike's work that it lacks lightness. The answer, and the explanation, is simple. This is, that it is almost impossible to bring together enough Merrymount books, outside the office of the Press, to form a fair judgment of their style and character. The books that are available elsewhere are those done for regular publishers and those issued by the Press itself. Both of these classes call for ordinary, simple books to be read. The more interesting commissions, typographically and decoratively, are those executed for private individuals, who wish a small edition for distribution among personal friends, and who expect to pay for elaboration. Books of this sort have from the first formed a large part of the output of the Press. It is only by accidental good fortune that any of these find their way into libraries or into the hands of those who collect fine printing. In such as have been examined, restraint and a scrupulous avoidance of anything that increases the cost beyond the legitimate requirements of the task in hand, are equally characteristic of the output. On the other hand, in these private issues, title-borders, head- and tail-pieces, floriated initials, and other typographic incidentals, appear frequently and prove that the printer knows how to use them effectively.

There is one other class of work that disposes of any notion that Updike cannot meet his rivals in the field of decorative adornment. This is the "job" printing which has always had an important place in the daily work of his Press. Programs, club notices, book-plates, advertising circulars or announcements, anything which ought to catch the eye and hold the attention, give the printer his finest opportunities for the use of imagination and for proof of his understanding of what can be done with the resources of type-cases. Updike was one of the first to perceive the great importance of the modern movement toward the use of printing to serve the purposes of commercial advertising, and he has manifested a controlled skill in utilizing every trick of type and ornament for meeting its legitimate demands. The occasional examples of work of this sort which come to view reveal a lightness of touch, a fertility of imagination, a sureness in adapting typographical material so as to secure desired effects, that are the fundamental characteristics of a great craftsman.

Updike's mastery of his business was recognized in 1911, when he was asked to conduct a course of instruction for students of printing in the Graduate School of Business Administration in Harvard University. This was part of a program of study, arranged by that School and supported by a group composed largely of members of the Boston Society of Printers, which it was hoped would develop into a permanent provision for training young men who planned to enter the printing industries. For five years, until the War put an end to the effort, he held the title of Lecturer on the Technique of Printing, and gave each year a series of talks on type-design and on the ways types have been used at different times in various countries. He put into these lectures all that he had learned during his European visits as well as at his Boston desk. His unceasing search for ideas had taken him to the old book-shops and the libraries as well as to the type-foundries, and he now had the incentive to bring his information together in orderly arrangement. This material, clarified by the classroom presentation, which luckily ceased before it became deaden-ing, was put into permanent form after the teaching ended and was published by the Harvard University Press in two volumes entitled *Printing Types*. This treatise established the author as a scholar of the first rank. It is a work of exten-sive learning based on thorough research, set forth without a trace of pedantry. It is written with much care, but the limi-tations of the subject make portions of it somewhat heavy. The author had a better chance to show his literary skill in a group of essays, *In the Day's Work*. Holding strictly to the subject of the printer's relation to his daily occupation, these essays have an ease of diction and a charm of style of very high quality.

Pre-eminent as a printer and the author of a scholarly work of recognized merit, Updike has done one other thing which, in the last analysis, is likely to be regarded as his most impor-tant service to cultural evolution. He has demonstrated that there is a steady demand for the best obtainable printing. Opinions may differ about his typography and about his judgments concerning the history and the use of type-faces. There can, however, be no gainsaying the fact that from 1893 until some date still in the future, his Merrymount Press pros-pered as a business enterprise, without once departing from its purpose of producing nothing that does not possess high technical excellence. Other presses, notably the Chiswick, can claim the right to have their record compared with this, but none can show so long a period of undeviating maintenance of an equal standard. To have done this without subsidy or any commercial support except that of its own customers, is to prove that there is a public demand for well-printed books and a readiness to make fine printing profitable.

FRAGMENTS OF MEMORY

―――――

RUDOLPH RUZICKA

―――――

A MONG the many illuminating quotations in Updike's conversation and writing, Sir Walter Raleigh's "Write, and
... you write yourself down whether you will or no" is at this
moment uppermost in my mind. The following paragraphs
about one who wrote and printed himself down so effectively
have become, I find, unconsciously autobiographical. They
were prompted by memories of a continuous friendship of
long standing and they are personal; however much he stressed
traditions and forms, Updike sought and valued above all
things the basic realities of human relationship, sincerity, truth,
and affection.

FIRST MEETINGS

OUR first meeting took place at the Hotel Lafayette in New
York in 1907. I was recommended to Updike by Lewis Hatch
for the engraving of a title-page decoration intended for a
volume of *The Humanists' Library*. I liked the "manuscript"
of the design, which later proved to be by Dwiggins, and
undertook the reproduction, carefully instructed by Updike
as to the character of line and the feeling that were to be preserved. Though not much feeling remained when I finished
the work, the engraving was finally accepted and used. But
my first meeting with Updike ended in a spirited disagree-
ment; the argument, I believe, concerned a question of contemporary art. Updike was then in his Renaissance mood and
I thought him arrogantly opinionated.

Two or three years later I made my first visit to Boston in
company with a friend. Our main purpose was to see Dwiggins, whom we found working in his studio on the concave
side of Cornhill. I had brought with me a portfolio of a dozen

of my engravings; wood-engraving was little practiced at the time—it was certainly unsung. These "original" engravings then I took to show Updike at the Merrymount Press in Summer Street (having advised with Dwiggins as to the wisdom of doing so) and to my surprise, at this second meeting, I found quite a different man, simple, appreciative, pertinently critical; flattering in that he showed me his own work.

Thus began my friendship with a man almost twice my age and, as he then seemed to me, ten times more experienced and clever than I. What made our relations easy was the fact, I suppose, that I was not "on the make" and was not a "brilliant bore," to use his favorite phrases. My admiration for his work and a desire to understand it helped as did perhaps the divergent character of our backgrounds.

At that time Updike strongly emphasized the genealogical and the social; to many he must have seemed a kind of walking Debrett and Social Register combined. Early in our acquaintance I remember listening patiently, in my workroom on Lexington Avenue, to a detailed account of a fashionable person of his social world. In a fit of youthful sincerity I said something to the effect that he was too accomplished a man to make so much fuss about what did not appear to me important; he did not bite my head off as I half expected but apologized disarmingly, saying: "That is the way I was brought up." Later when I was privileged to meet some of these friends they turned out to be real and wholly delightful people. Yet another remark of mine, provoked in argument and made in a state of premature "modernism," that he abandon the use of borrowed historical ornament, was ignored in charitable silence. Such friendly impertinences and misunderstandings were not too many and in the end helped clear the air for us both. Foundations of a friendship and later foundations of another kind were laid. He sent me at intervals of time a pound of Ceylon tea, a box of Castile soap, and a copy of the Book of Common Prayer. With the last came a note: "Having sent you Tea, Soap and the Prayer Book, you are now provided with the Foundations of Anglo-Saxon Culture."

HIS WORK

UPDIKE regarded his work as the lesser achievement of his life; the greater one was the overcoming of obstacles which made the work, and normal existence itself, possible. He said and wrote exactly what he thought and felt about his printing and its aims, and about much else, sometimes with an effect of understatement. A self-supporting printer, and not as some thought a man of private means who contrived with John Bianchi's magical aid to do professional work well, he accepted any job suited to the carefully limited range of the equipment of his Press. The results of his work he judged not according to the importance of the subject but according to the success of his solution of it, an attitude common in many other professions. If laymen, confused by the glitter of names and texts, caused Updike some irritation, they must be thanked for provoking many sallies of his mordant wit.

Updike took intense interest in everybody and everything, except mechanics, connected with his work. To his customers he was helpful not only with the rare materials of the Press but with what was more rare, his solid realism, wide learning, and disciplined taste. From the friends of the Press he accepted any reasonable suggestion, not at all adamant in matters relating to detail of design. To his friends he would send specimens of work in progress, especially of that relating to the Press, never failing when opportunity offered to display his latest products, often with undisguised pleasure in book, pamphlet, or label considered well done. He was proud of happy solutions of problems remote from what is commonly called fine printing, but no undue stress was laid on the obviously practical; it is almost certain that the master of The Merrymount was never astonished by those periodic discoveries, that type should be "easy to read," or that printing should be "invisible."

METHODS AND MECHANICS

IN *In the Day's Work* and elsewhere Updike said all he cared to say and perhaps all that need be said about his approach to the designing of a piece of printing. What he did not describe, though amply demonstrated, was the quality of his amazing knowledge of the intellectual and artistic tools of his profession. I have often seen him identify at a glance the precise style and size of a type, the subject immediately dismissed with an abrupt comment on the artistic values involved in its use. This knowledge appeared instinctive; there was never the slightest suggestion of the erudite drudge — his perception had the quality of genius.

The processes he employed in laying-out his work were almost entirely mental; he never attempted to sketch or in any but the roughest way indicate the actual type. The design was formed in his mind, the size of type and its disposition often indicated on the copy; thenceforth corrections and adjustments, never too many, were made on successive proofs. He never agreed to show his lay-outs in public exhibitions. When I asked him to contribute such material for the Century Club exhibition of "Stages in Design and Technique of Book-making" he sent only some marked proofs, but with them a model exhibit of galley-proofs demonstrating the vigilant expertness of his proof-readers. Updike did not believe that technical processes were of any real interest or value to the general public; there was a time when he strongly disapproved of exhibiting books, which he claimed must be handled to be fully appreciated.

He had no talent whatever for the mechanics of printing, and betrayed this lack when writing the technical parts of both *Printing Types* and *Some Aspects of Printing Old and New*. "No one," he wrote at the time he worked on *Printing Types*, "was ever more interested in the results of the work of a printing-press than I am; and I am sure that nobody who was so much interested, ever knew so little about the workings of the machinery. To me all machinery is like a hideous form of algebra. Two and two, in machines, do *not* make four to my mind with the slightest conviction; and when people say 'you see this cog fits into that, the result is so and so,' I never do see why there should be that result. . . . If the machine that casts type should suddenly cast animals for Noah's ark, it would seem to me just as natural and nothing to be surprised at!"

A visitor taken through the works of the Press, always too hastily, must have been struck by the master's indifference to the presses and type-cases passed by as though they did not belong to him. The exception was the proof-readers' room, of the efficiency and scholarly furnishing of which Updike was justifiably proud. This was the learned heart of the works and it is safe to assume that no "Indigo" Jones ever got by.

The *Description of The Merrymount Press* is really a catalogue of exhibits and decorations. These were strung along all the walls so their owner, one sometimes thought, would never be left with only machinery to look at and talk about.

LECTURES AND WRITING

UPDIKE's motto should have been *Volo, ergo sum*. His infrequent public talks were the result of sheer will power. One of the first was given at the Club of Odd Volumes in 1912 and that, he confessed, "scared me almost to death." The talk resulted in an offer to him from a publishing house to write a book on the history and aesthetics of typography; "an elegant compliment" he thought; and he straightway though privately proposed the following announcement for a book that would, he wrote to me, "deceive the Elect and be hard to Read":

Now Ready

TEN TALKS ON TYPE
BEING A CONSIDERATION OF
PRINCIPLES OF TONE-HARMONY
IN RELATION TO MEDIAEVAL LETTER FORMS
PRECEDED BY A FOREWORD ON THE
IDEALISM OF HEGEL IN ITS RELATION TO
THE ALPHABET

Some of the lectures on the Technique of Printing delivered to the Graduate School of Business Administration of Harvard University took place at the Press in Summer Street, but they could hardly have been called public. In the one I was invited to hear, on French type-forms of the fifteenth century, he showed no assurance whatever of manner, however well he controlled the matter. His last lectures delivered to the Friends of the Harvard College Library were done with more ease and even some enjoyment.

There was much revision of the first Harvard lectures before their publication in *Printing Types*, as well as of the last ones collected in *Some Aspects of Printing*. The technical parts of the former especially caused Updike acute agony and he thought seriously of omitting the chapter on type-casting which at first seemed to him, and to others as well, "terribly wooden." The book, he felt, became cumulatively better as it went on, for the reason that the periods of the eighteenth and nineteenth centuries interested him much more than the technical matter and the periods of the incunabula.

His shorter papers too were written with the utmost care and regard for balance and interest. The several personal memoirs of his friends were done with comparative ease, an unpublished one of Mrs. Wharton with great feeling and dash, and without any alteration whatever.

Updike had a great fear of dullness and exaggeration. He guarded against the former by resort to quotation, needlessly it seemed to me; there was in his theoretical writing an over-simplification of the aesthetic due to his horror of the gushing faddist and to his meticulous sense of proportion.

ANNUAL KEEPSAKES

THE series of my engravings of New Year's cards begun in 1911 and sent to the Friends of The Merrymount Press were originally proposed by John Bianchi. The subject was often suggested by Updike himself, and sometimes he would come with me while I made the sketch—pouring out his intimate and highly entertaining knowledge of places and people. Thus I came to know the furnishing and the inmates of a kitchen in a house on Beacon Hill, and the history of, and an anecdote about, the weather-vane on top of Faneuil Hall. My chief concern however was with the designs and their execution and of this I could never convince a distinguished lady who more than once reproached me for engraving "too many red brick churches."

The Latin inscriptions, almost always apt (I could never agree, however, that *Arabia Deserta* was applicable to Worcester Square), often pointed, sometimes humorously puzzling, were Updike's special care. Here again my interest was largely formal and technical. Lettering is harder to engrave than portraits; everyone knows the physiognomy of letters and is a critical relative, most of all of course the great historian of type-faces for whom the engravings were made.

CONTEMPORARIES AND VISITORS

To HIS contemporaries Updike was generously appreciative. He greatly admired the work of Bruce Rogers, keenly aware of Rogers' artistic training and technical mastery. Nothing pleased him so much as the unmatched summary of the work of the Merrymount Press written by Rogers, anonymously, in an article entitled "Modern Printing in the United States" and published in the Printing Number of the *London Times* on September 10, 1912. The notice was afterwards effectively used in *The Work of The Merrymount Press*, with Updike's introduction. I felt at the time that in this pamphlet, with the redundant Lethaby quotation, too much was made of "common sense." When I pointed this out to Updike he partly agreed: "People are so dull sometimes that it does no harm to say the same thing over again in another way." He had too a high regard for Carl Rollins, who he said "had the advantage of being a professional printer," and for what Rollins achieved at and with the Yale University Press. As to New York and "places of that kind" — as described on a humorous map of The Hub he sent me one Christmas — Updike liked best the work of John Fass done at the Harbor Press.

A hesitant visitor who came to The Merrymount Press expecting to find "a mixture of King Solomon in wisdom and a wild-cat in manner," to quote his words, discovered a normal human being. Updike was cordial to anyone he considered a real printer or a "real person," but an Elbert Hubbard attempting to crash the gates as "one master-printer calling upon another" found himself non-existent. The excessively curious likewise met with scant welcome, especially where equipment of any sort belonging to or being used by the Press was the object of curiosity. Such material Updike considered strictly private; its acquisition was the result of his foresight, effort, and wit, its provenance a carefully guarded secret.

His relation to Cleland, Dwiggins, and myself, apart from decorative work ordered for definite purposes and which had of necessity to conform to specifications, was one of complete respect; he wrote willingly and appreciatively of our divers efforts at certain stages of our development. When I asked him if he had any suggestions to make regarding my handling of the engravings for *Newark* (with perhaps a faint echo of the "book beautiful" in my mind), he replied "it was the printer's job to serve the material handed him, not the other way about."

LITERATURE AND ART

Updike's alert and sensitive mind absorbed a wide range of knowledge which he shared with me with the joy of a personal discovery, as of one who never "had it" in school. He gained an especially close acquaintance with eighteenth- and nineteenth-century English literature, English history, and French seventeenth- and eighteenth-century letters and memoirs. Of later writers, Jane Austen, Trollope, and the more modern Hardy seemed to appeal to him most. I know that he did not like Shaw, for I was made to serve as a vehicle of Updike's disapproval of the brilliant dramatist, in an article which he wrote on my work. The contemporary writers, French, English and American, he followed closely though some of the latest in natural puzzlement.

While he often quoted Emerson he had little liking for the dissentient and high-thinking Concord. Of Thoreau, I only heard him repeat the alleged Concord gossip, that the great individualist relieved his loneliness at Walden Pond by frequent and secret visits to the village to buy supplies of pie. But he put up the most fitting monument to Thoreau, in a Latin inscription on a Keepsake of the Press: "Cato said he would rather be asked why not than why a statue should be erected to him."

Although strongly influenced by Santayana he did not always agree with the philosopher. When in one of their conversations Santayana deplored the plainness of Boston and other American towns Updike mildly objected: "Yet Boston is 'the loveliest ... of the plain'." In later years Updike profited from his reading of Croce, whose wise lines about "the impossibility of resting on the results of past thought" he quoted in his last book. About Cortissoz, whom he always admired, I once heard him exclaim: "Lord, how I wish there were more critics like him!" For less able and less kindly critics, himself penetratingly critical, he preserved tolerant silence.

Early in the unquiet progress of our acquaintance when I attempted to talk about Tolstoy or Ibsen, I do not remember which, Updike called me "Gothic" — he did not share my interest in what he called "heavy" poetry, drama, and music.

More than one writer has remarked how slightly Updike was influenced by William Morris' printing. He had in fact no real sympathy for the Arts and Crafts movement and compared the extreme manifestations of its "sincerity" to the sincerity of the amateur actor who, preparing to play the part of Othello, "blackened himself all over." He had no respect for manual labor as such in deceptive contrast to his dislike of machinery — to him both were means to an end merely — he valued the accomplished in the arts.

The enthusiast who had just discovered "a minor master of the wrong century" did not upset him but may in turn have been upset by Updike's knowledge and ready wit. Updike's views were balanced, though by no means conventional; qualities of color and design in works of art of any period were keenly observed and noted. His sensitiveness to color and design is revealed in his work. This work, intended to be "*so agreeable to its purpose as to appear inevitable*" (Updike's words and italics) was based not only on an "unerring sense of style" (as Rogers put it) but on his native practicality. A strong sense of the downright utilitarian helped to carry him safely through the varying "periods" of the time in which he lived and through the immense riches of the library in which he worked.

CONVERSATION

UPDIKE's conversation with me was unreserved and covered many subjects. He liked to talk about Spain, fascinated by that explosive mixture of the mystical and the earthly; and about religion, in which he seemed at one time on the edge of a conversion. The unquestioned authority of his liturgical printing only partly expressed his deep knowledge of and interest in the outward forms of faith.

He was warmest in recollections springing from the regions of his origin, wherein lay his deepest affections, and most animated in his talk about people. However charitable at heart, he did not always have a "charitable eye and ear," though he displayed the light touch in his comments—as for example on a loquacious friend of great industry who "worked all night and talked about it all day" or on one of roving habits, quoting a French satirist: "plus ça change, plus c'est la même chose." Like Hazlitt, he liked his friends better for having faults that he could talk about.

Despite the profound admiration he had for England, to which he owed so much, Updike was inclined to be critical of the visiting Englishman—rather like a jealous relation. To English women—and women generally—he showed more patience. To one, puzzled by the lack of "privacy" in New England towns, he carefully explained: "There are three reasons for the lack: 1. *Historical*—The early settlers were in danger of Indians and for protection were obliged to live close together; 2. *Moral*—Sometime in the nineteenth century a misguided though well-intentioned clergyman invented the thing called 'community spirit' whereupon most fences were pulled down; 3. *Horticultural*—Owing to rigors of climate, privet does not grow high enough in New England." Such encounters with those expressing foreign points of view were faithfully and often gleefully reported.

The broader, and amusing, sides of his work were talked about, but seldom "shop" and business, except in my shop or his office; these subjects were completely ruled out at lunch or the dinner hour.

There was however in later years a marked relaxation in most respects, due partly to his pleasure in the mounting appreciation of his work both at home and abroad. He felt at ease among men of his profession, at the meetings of the Society of Printers, and, as I last saw him outside his house and office, with the casual and warm-hearted Typophiles. But he did not easily suffer the business of being celebrated. In his clear-sighted way he knew that the substance of creative life is the planning and the doing, not the collected result. Therefore the sad introspective note in his speech at the time the American Institute of Graphic Arts and the Grolier Club opened their comprehensive and splendid exhibition of the work of the Merrymount Press:

"A distinguished member of the teaching staff of Harvard University once said to me, that as he looked back on his life, it seemed to him nothing more than a confused getting ready to begin. It seems so to me, as I look at the books shown in this exhibition, and realize that they are the result of a lifetime of work. Sometimes I ask myself, 'Is this all that we at the Merrymount Press have accomplished? If we could have begun with the knowledge that we have now!' For I am not one of those who consider long life necessarily a matter for congratulation. It may be that it is allotted chiefly to those who have been slow in learning their lesson — like the dull pupil kept after school. Alas, by the time we get our training in life and in work, we are whisked away to some other part of the universe for which we faintly hope that our experiences here may have prepared us. That all this discipline cannot be pure waste is, perhaps, a convincing argument for immortality."

As A human being Updike seemed to me happiest when away from things of his own arranging. In such moments there descended upon him a kind of serenity, when he talked and listened with an air of untroubled peace; and that is the way I like to remember him.

THE SOUL OF
THE MERRYMOUNT PRESS

DAVID T. POTTINGER

NEARLY forty years ago a young employee of the Riverside Press in Cambridge decided, as young men sometimes do, to go into business for himself. It was a propitious
moment. When he had entered Houghton Mifflin's Boston
office twelve years earlier, the shadows of the great American
literary dynasty were still visible; probably Emerson, Longfellow, Whittier, and Lowell were often announced by the
young clerk in the outer room. By the end of his apprenticeship America was crossing a new threshold, into a period
when artistic and literary influences were much more cos-
mopolitan. The nineties had begun; and William Morris,
though near the close of his career, was the apostle of a renaissance. After Morris had applied his vigorous talents to the
manufacture of furniture, textiles, wall-papers, and a dozen
other commodities, he had made himself a master of printing
and book-designing. His influence immediately brought about
an alteration in typography comparable only to the revival
of Caslon types at the Chiswick Press some fifty years before.
When, therefore, Berkeley Updike made up his mind to leave
the Riverside Press, the world was aware of the fact that
printing could be made much more beautiful than it had been
in the recent past.

He chose the name of Merrymount (familiar to him from
one of Hawthorne's *Twice Told Tales*) for his new venture
because that famous spot had represented an enviable mingling
of work and pleasure. Except as a neat symbol of Morris'
doctrines, there is no significance in the name, Mr. Updike's
family having been Rhode Islanders from the beginning.

At first the work was confined to designing and laying-out
jobs, the actual composition and press-work being contracted

for with manufacturing printers. This arrangement is common enough in our own day when type is often the last thing you will find in a "typographer's studio," but in 1893 it must have been surprising. If so, it was the first of a long series of surprises Mr. Updike had in store. The next came when he went to Europe, searched around in the old-established foundries of England and the continent for good but neglected type-faces, procured hand-made papers from an ancient mill in northern Italy, and returned to America with a first-hand knowledge of what European printers were doing. He has ever refused to be content with the second-hand or the derivative; he has gone directly to the sources in a way that indicates both a scholarly mind and a shrewd business sense. Still another surprise came when he abandoned the "artistic" neighborhood of Beacon Hill for quarters in the modern loft-building at 232 Summer Street. One can almost hear the shocked murmurs, "Can any art come out of the South Cove?" but once again a sound business sense dictated a course that time has amply justified.

All these things which, as I say, must have astonished the dilettantes of the nineties, continue to puzzle the aesthetes of our own time; for all of them have failed to comprehend what Mr. Updike has been about. Over and over again he has insisted that he is running a business, not an art museum. He points to his power-driven presses and his machine-made papers. He mentions, albeit in a low tone, cost sheets and accounting systems. But the prejudiced will have none of it; convinced that there is something artful and craftful on the premises, they make much ado over the matter. If they were right, the Merrymount Press would now be lying alongside the dozens of other "private presses" that have been born and have faded away since the days of the Kelmscott Press. The truth is much simpler. Mr. Updike is a rare combination of artist and business man, and he has an infinite perseverance. Year after year he has gone on, printing to the best of his ability, steeping himself in the history of his craft, refusing to draw any circle prematurely, and keeping his eye fixed on the far gain. Nevertheless, as in the case of the man whom Boswell mentions, cheerfulness has continually crept in, and the significance of the Maypole of Merrymount has never been lost.

One aspect of it is to be found in the comely and dignified offices in which the Press is conducted. The visitor opens a door into a well-lighted room, the walls of which are hung with rare type-founders' specimen sheets and engraved portraits of famous printers. On the right and left are arched glass doors which were once windows opening onto the balcony of the old Boston Museum. That on the left leads into the accounting department; that on the right into the reception room. Engravings and old mahogany give this room an air of dignity far different from the places where most printers receive their customers. A highboy against one wall contains a collection of valuable wood-cuts, many of them engraved by the Bewicks at the end of the eighteenth century. On the other wall is a show-case in which are exhibited recent productions of the shop. Next to this room is Mr. Updike's office. Here is one of the finest typographical libraries in this country. The collector's envy is divided between the cases containing a virtually complete file of Merrymount books and, on the other hand, the cases that house Mr. Updike's library of specimen books which one authority has declared to be "probably unrivalled in private hands." Beyond are the usual working quarters, the composing- and press-rooms and the proofroom. Even here, however, the walls are hung with appropriate engravings, portraits, and photographs, many of them the gifts of famous people.

This is really a small establishment, considering the amount and variety of work the Press turns out each year. Perhaps, however, it may point a moral to those printers who tie up disproportionate amounts of capital in freakish type-faces that speedily become obsolete. At any rate, Mr. Updike has confined himself largely to types that have long proved their worth, and by his skill in using them he has produced the effect of ever-fresh variety. First in line, of course, is Caslon, the sturdy English type designed early in the eighteenth century after certain fine Dutch models. Then there is Scotch, a sound face dating from the beginning of the nineteenth century. Between there is the Oxford type, a transitional face which originated over a century ago in the Philadelphia type foundry of Binny & Ronaldson and which has long been a favorite with Mr. Updike. Besides these, there is a comparatively new type, the Lutetia, cut a few years ago by the distinguished Dutchman, Dr. J. van Krimpen, and finally a Dutch seventeenth-century type called Janson, which has been used in the new Standard Prayer Book and in a number of other recent Merrymount books. It is strong yet delicately modeled, clear and sharp as Garamond and yet much more allied to the Fell types, which also are of Dutch origin. From the early period of the Press come the two special types, Merrymount and Montallegro, the first designed by Bertram Grosvenor Goodhue and the second by Herbert P. Horne. Then there are, naturally, smaller fonts of initials and of occasional types, appropriate for display lines on title-pages and elsewhere. Fleurons, ornaments, borders, are there in plenty, especially from the French and English foundries of the eighteenth century. Only Baskerville among the great historic types seems, curiously, to be lacking.

So much for the means; the result may be observed in the small but thoroughly representative exhibition now [1931] set up in Goodspeed's Book Shop on Ashburton Place. Most of the volumes have been selected from recent work because the intention has been to show the Merrymount Press of the present rather than to give an historical survey of its accomplishment. The visitor will at once be struck by the variety, richness, and high quality of the books. Every format, from the modest duodecimo to the stately folio, is at hand. The bindings run the whole gamut from severely sober to gaily decorative. There are books with black and white illustrations and others with colored collotypes. In some, the ornament and embellishment attract the eye, while in others there is nothing but plain type and paper. Not since the extensive exhibition of the American Institute of Graphic Arts in New

York in 1928 has it been possible to get so vivid an idea of the astonishing range of Merrymount printing.

For the personal touch one must first spend a little time over the early circulars and announcements. At the distance of forty years they are just old enough to awaken reminiscences. What days those were when we first began to realize that beauty could become, even in New England, an integral part of life. What names rush to our minds: Bertram Goodhue, Will Bradley, Carl Heintzemann, Copeland & Day, and dozens of other brave companions from the time when to be young was very heaven, and we all were young! But why be wistful over the departed years when present maturity proves that it has more than fulfilled the promise of youth?

Lest your eyes dazzle with the magnificence of the liturgical books, let them become accustomed to those done for commercial publishers: Robert Frost's *West Running Brook;* Henry Dwight Sedgwick's *Pro Vita Monastica;* Thomas Hardy's *Three Wayfarers;* La Fontaine's *Fables;* George S. Bryan's *The Ghost in the Attic.* These books, it is evident to even the least critical buyer, are far better than the average. Their paper and type, it will be found on examination, are pretty much the same as other printers use. Their delightful ornaments begin to add the note of distinction, their harmonious bindings intensify that note, but their charm is still otherwhere. They are pleasant just because they satisfy one's instinct for what is "right" in a book. We like them, in other words, even though we may not know why we like them. Doesn't their secret lie in the subtle but evident respect with which the printer approached his job? Here are not so many words to be stuck down on paper by the first handy means; here are thoughts which someone has deemed worthy of preservation, thoughts which were the object of care on the author's part and which demand equal care from the printer.

In the same category, almost, are the "privately printed" books such as those done for the Club of Odd Volumes, the Carteret Book Club, the Grolier Club, the Quarto Club, and individuals. In these instances Mr. Updike has evidently been less hampered by the necessity of working within an appropriation, and so he has been able to indulge in rather more decoration, with time enough to see that it becomes an integral part of the whole. Often, too, the format is of a shape and size that seem to do more complete justice to the text but that would not be welcome on the book-seller's standardized shelf.

Among these privately-printed books one may well pick out and ponder over Caspar Whitney's life of Charles Adelbert Canfield, which has just been finished. It is set in Bodoni, a type which called forth the most violent fulminations from William Morris. It is Bodoni properly used, with wide leading, more than ample margins, brilliant press-work, hard paper. Bodoni himself could not have improved upon it. It is a complete answer to those who vaguely connect the Merrymount Press with *fin de siècle* aesthetics.

Some eight or ten of the books may be grouped together because they deliberately seek quaintness. In such volumes as *Pineapples of Finest Flavour, The Journal of Lady Louisa Stewart*, the diary and the letters of Mrs. Amory, and a few others, the printer was obliged to reproduce as well as he could in type those calligraphic abbreviations dear to the eighteenth century, the superior letters in words like "M^{rs.}" the interlining and correcting of hastily written manuscripts. Caslon type and a wide quarto page meet these requirements. On the other hand, when Mr. Updike aims at quaintness of another sort, such as "Walter" Whitman's temperance novel of the 1840's, *Franklin Evans*, he can just as easily turn the trick by different means.

Practical printers will gaze with envy at some volumes which represent the overcoming of difficult technical problems. How, for instance, could anyone hope to make a more dignified and suitable book than the record of those who contributed to the endowment fund for Sulgrave Manor? The "copy" consisted of thousands of names arranged alphabetically and geographically! Or consider the catalogues of the Bullard Collection and of the John Carter Brown Library. The obstacles they presented can be appreciated only by those who have tried to lay out a catalogue or a bibliography. Again, imagine the originals of *Nailer Tom's Diary*, which was included among the "Fifty Best" of 1930—a mass of old notebooks, full of misspellings, bad punctuation, dull remarks on the weather, all reproduced faithfully, attractively, and compactly.

All this, however, is but the foil to the crown of the exhibit, the group of magnificent liturgical books. Among them, as a sort of opening door, I include the *Glebe House Book*, which consists of about a hundred pages each divided off by red lines into twenty-two spaces for the entry of visitors' names. The headings are set in black letter and Caslon, with a coat-of-arms in red. The title-page shows its purpose: "The Book of Remembrance, Being a Record of Visitors to the Glebe House or Parsonage at Woodbury, Connecticut, the Birthplace of American Episcopacy." Richly decorative but admirably suited to its use, the volume makes one wonder why even our best clubs content themselves with drab "registers."

Aesthetically as well as chronologically, the whole history of the Merrymount Press lies between the new Prayer Book and the *Altar Book* of 1896. The drawings of Robert Anning Bell and the borders and initials of Bertram Grosvenor Goodhue contribute to the magnificence of the *Altar Book*. In fact the Kelmscott point of view was so strong in the mid-nineties that no one would have ventured to lay out such a volume in any other fashion. It is no derogation of Morris to say that his typography is no longer ours; his books will always stand very high, and along with them will be the *Altar Book* as the best American representative of the same aesthetic impulses.

Mr. Updike's progress in ecclesiastical printing is indicated by *The Ordinary and Canon of the Mass Together with the Order for the Administration of the Lord's Supper or Holy Communion, and the Holy Chant*, issued in 1913. It is set in Goodhue's Merrymount type, and the format is a large folio. The rich pages of the service, where the effects are due solely to the proper use of type and to the rubrication, are much more satisfactory from a typographical point of view than the earlier work, and the pages of music are as gorgeous as anyone could demand.

Another fifteen years brings us to the lovely duodecimo containing the consecration service for the chapel at St. George's School. The page is small because each person in the congregation was to hold the book in his hand, and a large size of type was selected so that everyone might easily read the text or find his place. The type is Janson, the same as that used later in the Prayer Book. Since every page or pair of pages has rubrication, the presswork could by no means have been an easy job.

Finally, then, we come to the gem of the exhibition and one of the few superb books of modern printing history, the official edition of the new *Standard Book of Common Prayer of the Protestant Episcopal Church in the United States of America*, printed through the generosity of J. Pierpont Morgan. Shall we give the higher praise to the simple but ingenious arrangement of the Calendar or to the dignified pages of the Psalter? Whatever the problems connected with the former, one must remember that even the pages of the services were fraught with difficulties because the printer was required to set each one in such fashion that it could be reproduced page for page in smaller type and a different format so that the turning of pages in the chancel would synchronize with the turning of pages in the pews. This important detail was but one of the many practical questions of liturgiology which Mr. Updike solved through his extensive knowledge of ecclesiastical history and practice.

Before the great Prayer Book both printer and reader stand silent with admiration. In the presence of the finished work we can pass by with the merest mention the long months of toil it required, the selection and casting of the special types, the many experiments to secure the right quality of paper, the difficulties of composition, the constant oversight to assure perfection of press-work. All these are memories of the past, like the scaffolding no longer needed around a completed work of architecture. Only one cannot forget the devotion and loyalty of the workmen of the Merrymount Press, and especially of the junior partner, Mr. John Bianchi.

One's attention comes back again and again to the details of the book itself—the pulsating crimson of the rubrication, the clearness of the type, the gracefulness of the large initials, the sharpness of impression, the harmony of paper and text, and the gorgeous crimson binding. It is truly a magnificent book, calm in its glory, unobtrusive in its richness. Not a single bit of ornament has been used; the whole effect is due to the impeccable use of type, ink, and paper. It will stand as the finest product of the American press in our time, a high-water mark to indicate that in one art, at least, we can attain beauty through dignity and simplicity.

Those who know Mr. Updike will further see in the Prayer Book an expression of his personality; for no man can lay his hand to a piece of work without revealing himself. A glance at the trial pages which three other printers submitted to the Prayer Book Committee before the contract was awarded, would make this fact even more evident. The Prayer Book according to the revision of 1928 is far from being the casual product of a good printing establishment; it is the crowning achievement of a man whose life has tended to this goal. A great printer was given the opportunity to do a great book, and he did it. [Curtain calls, now? Mr. Updike will not respond! He is at his desk, working at the next job!] Nor shall friendship do more than hint of winter evenings when the conversation has raced merrily before the fireplace in his house on Marlborough Street, or those long summer afternoons at Hopewell Green when we have gazed across the sunlit valley to the purpling line of the Vermont hills. Such are the materials of biography; the task now is to make some appraisal of these Merrymount books and the means by which they are produced.

The distinguishing mark of them all is to be found in a high seriousness tempered by an urbane humor. Each has been looked at as a problem to be solved according to its own requirements and not as just another job to be turned out according to a hastily-chosen formula. Type and especially ornament have been selected in accordance with the spirit of the author's words and never for the sake of prettifying the page. Every detail of arrangement, paper, and binding has been the result of thought. Press forms have never been passed as "good enough"; they must be as nearly perfect as the press-man can make them. Hence every book looks as if it had been made by a man who knew what he was about. Every-where is evidence of the master's hand, unobtrusive yet firm. Control, discipline, knowledge, maintain a rigid standard of work.

Obviously these results can be reached only in small-scale production closely superintended by a man of trained artistic judgment and with an almost automatic technical skill based upon years of exacting experience. Mr. Updike has been will-ing to learn his craft historically, theoretically, and practically; and he has had the intellectual curiosity to become acquainted with a wide range of other interests that create a background for his practice. His authoritative history of printing types, his delightful essays on the printer's daily work, his edition of Rowe Mores' book on the English type founders, and his various articles in *The Fleuron* are not only permanent con-tributions to the literature of printing but they are evidence of his wide knowledge of world literature and art. His honor-ary degree from Harvard was a recognition of his scholarship as well as of his pre-eminence in printing.

Furthermore, Mr. Updike has never been content to run his business by the modern method of delegated authority. He watches closely every step in the manufacture of a book and is willing to spend long hours at his desk. The bridge table, the golf course, the convention junket, and the night club — all those things that are so essential to Mr. Babbitt's big busi-ness—have had no part in building up the reputation of the Merrymount Press. Fun there has been, but of the sort that was current before our sudden wealth outmoded Benjamin Franklin's precepts of diligence and thrift. The cost may seem high to those who can attend to business only between the moments of distraction; yet it is the only successful alternative to mass production. Pragmatically, too, it has been demonstrated to be a wise method; for in these days of economic depression, when the printing business is especially hard hit, the Merrymount Press is busier than ever and can foresee no slackening of its output.

To scorn delights and live laborious days in obedience to one's own loftiest purposes has ever been the foundation for an abiding fame and an enduring influence. Mr. Updike must gain a solid satisfaction in seeing the result of his four decades of exacting work, even though he repeats the old motto with which he started, *"Optimum vix satis* — the best is scarcely good enough."* Printers of America, England, France, Germany, Italy, Denmark, Holland, and Spain recognize him as a master, perhaps the greatest master-printer of our time. And there can be no reasonable doubt that his fame is secure, not merely as the representative of printing in the first half of the twentieth century, but as the peer of the great typographers whose work he has so carefully studied and so faithfully carried on.

AN ENQUIRY INTO UPDIKE AND
THE NAME MERRYMOUNT

CARL PURINGTON ROLLINS

THE printing issued from the Merrymount Press has been
known to the public for half a century. It has been shown
in many exhibitions and it has been examined and appraised
by the critics. They have found in it numerous monuments as
well as a great deal of admirable straightforward craftsmanship; in all of it there is the same fundamentally sound conception of printing "good for its purpose," in the words of the
founder of the Press, Daniel Berkeley Updike. If a certain
maturity manifested itself as the years went on, yet in 1893
Updike knew very clearly what he wanted to do and how he
wanted to do it. This knowledge did not spring from any
fever of excitement or from any love of novelty. It was
rather a slow and orderly development in the comprehension
of typographic standards during a dozen years of close association with one of the most famous of American printing-
houses; and it was an attempt, like all good craftsmanship, to
bring to problems of the present the knowledge and understanding of the past.

It has been the habit of critics to regard the work of the
1870's and 1880's as negligible by modern typographic standards. It is true that the great Lower Level of printing was of
inferior merit: the types were thin and weak; the formats
suffered from anemia; the bindings were poor in design. But
also there were some printing houses which produced creditable books. One or two instances which are the more pertinent
because they may have fallen under the eye of the young
Updike may be mentioned. In 1864 Ticknor & Fields published George Ticknor's *Life of William Hickling Prescott.*
It is a solid quarto volume printed by the old firm of Welch,
Bigelow & Co., at their University Press in Cambridge. It is

set in a readable size of old-style type, within rules and with marginal notes, and, for perhaps the last time in America in the case of a serious work, the long ſ is used throughout. The title-page is in the best style of the period, but a little weak for modern taste; otherwise the book would be a very creditable piece of work for any present-day shop to turn out. In 1883 the Prince Society of Boston published as one of their regular series a reprint of Thomas Morton's *New English Canaan*. This again was printed at the University Press in Cambridge, in a modernized old-style of ample size. Both of these books had proper margins, impeccable type-setting, good paper, and careful, firm press-work. What went on at the University Press was also true at its next-door neighbor's, with whose work Updike was associated for twelve years, the Riverside Press. The book-work of the latter Press was a little less spectacular, but it possessed all the conservative typographic minutiae of the best printing of the time. Such a book as Hawthorne's *Our Old Home*, set in old-style type, is an excellent example. Child's *English and Scottish Popular Ballads*, issued in parts in the 80's and 90's is a careful and complex piece of type-setting; Lowell's *Essays* are done in octavo with modern roman in flawless if unemotional style.

These were the books which were issuing from the Cambridge presses in Updike's formative years. They were conventional, orderly, carefully set and printed. They had all the virtues of sound craftsmanship. If they lacked something in design, it may be pointed out that the Centennial Exposition of 1876 was an artistic horror, and that the World's Columbian Exposition, which then seemed so marvelous, was more notable for the first stirrings of a new sensitiveness in American aesthetics, than as an artistic summation.

All this would point out that the so-called Revival of Printing in England did not mean that all printing done even in America in the twenty-five years preceding was bad. And Updike, if he once succumbed to the antiquarianism of the moment in the *Altar Book*, or to its American echo in the pseudo-Colonialism of such a book as *In the Governor's*

Garden, had a more enduring training in the long and slowly evolving tradition of orthodox printing. It was this grounding which carried the superstructure of the Merrymount Press.

The year 1893 was an auspicious time to set up a Press, especially for a man who had a clear idea of what he wanted to do. But even for such a man there are better times and worse ones in which to begin. In 1893 the ferment of the revival of printing had reached America. The World's Columbian Exposition at Chicago had stimulated American interest in something else than the settlement of the West and the development of American business on a large scale. Sullivan's work at Chicago had roused our architects; the work of the Revival printers in England had stirred the younger aesthetes; young men in Boston and Cambridge were publishing new and exciting material in a new way; in every department of design there were interesting things stirring. Ten years before, the Press would have functioned in a vacuum; ten years later, it would have been too late to catch the flood tide at its beginning. And there was a definite commission for an *Altar Book* to be worked out with the brilliant young architect Goodhue. Updike had had a bitter lesson in his work on the Prayer Book of 1892: no further collaboration of that sort was thinkable — now his own office in which he could be his own master, his own type, a private face in the spirit of the times, and a book for the Church. Both then and later there were family friends whose support was unquestionably of value, but already he had begun to attract the notice of discriminating observers who saw in the young printer a promise of careful work of distinction "a little better than seems necessary."

Updike speaks rather blithely in *In the Day's Work* of the simple paraphernalia needed for designing printing — a quiet room, a large table, sheets of paper, and specimens of type. This is the way in which most modern books are planned, and it is the way in which Updike started out when he left Riverside. He had a quiet room, and no printing-office of his own. He found almost at once that the idea was too simple. He could only imperfectly control the printing-offices in which he had to place the composition and press-work. *The Hazard Family of Rhode Island*, although set up and printed in a first class Boston printing-house, is not of Merrymount Press quality. It illustrates the difficulties in securing the necessary degree of perfection by a system of remote control, after the design has issued from the ivory chamber. The ideal condition is for the designer and the craftsman to be one and the same; in default of such harmony, the next best thing is for the designer and the craftsman to work in immediate touch with each other. In Updike's case this meant, since he could not himself set type, the setting-up of a composing-room and later a press-room, and the engaging of suitable personnel. He had, it is true, already invested in the Altar Book type, but that book was a "sport," and a single font of type does not make a printing-office. A much more complicated equipment is necessary, and he was forced to provide himself with such helps. It was not a matter for him to enter into joyously; it entailed obligations even more perplexing than the employment of other printing-offices, but he knew that it was the only way in which he could secure the results he was after.

Once entered on the career of printer rather than book designer, there was no stopping until the final acquisition of presses and eventually of type-setting machines. The astuteness of the man is apparent in this very early realization of the necessity of having his own shop under his own immediate control.

Updike's career is an exemplification of "It's dogged as does it." However much he may have shrunk from the responsibilities of equipment and employees, he could not shrink from the urge to make his product as perfect as possible, and even the financial depression of a later time did not deter him from expansion to the logical size of a satisfactory establishment.

In the slow building up of such a business Updike was fortunate from the first in his choice of a foreman; in John Bianchi he found a man whose zeal and loyalty were invaluable, and whose technical training as a printer could supplement Updike's taste and knowledge. Printing is not a one-man craft, and to this fortunate association of two men of widely different talents much of the success of the Merrymount Press is due.

The equipment of the press was exceptional in one particular only. Machinery is machinery everywhere, but the type which Updike slowly accumulated became such as no other printing house in America ever possessed. Here Updike's discriminating taste and discerning eye, as well as his determination, were employed to the best advantage. Such places as the Riverside, the University, the DeVinne, the Gilliss presses had had a large and varied assortment of type, but it had not been selected with the rigorous exclusiveness of that of the Merrymount Press. The intrusion of type-setting machinery was inevitable, and when it came there was as inevitably a slight impairment of quality. This is not a sentimental regret for the old hand type, but a subtle reflection of certain inherent qualities in the machine itself. It would require too much space to go into this matter in detail, and after all, *autres temps, autres moeurs.*

The details of the printing process may change imperceptibly, but the requirements of good printing remain essentially unaltered. What matters, what has always mattered, is the printer, what manner of man he is. Updike never said much in public about his heritage, his private life, or his inner conflicts. A few restrained comments in his writings, with a sort of warning that they were all that was needed, contribute something. His unrecorded conversations, especially with women, to whom he found it easier to talk, and some revealing letters (many of them not now to be quoted) give further information. Something too can be deduced from the biographical facts of his life. His heritage was of New England for many generations; he was a "true Rhode Island man." From his earliest youth he was a reader. He became widely acquainted with literature, and his almost phenomenal memory is evident in his innumerable apt quotations. In fact there are almost too many of these quotations. They suggest a quality of his character which marked him as a man of talent rather than as a genius. His was not an original mind, but an observant and a retentive one, which enabled him to assemble his remarkable repertory of type and ornaments and to use them fittingly and effectively. Merrymount printing is not so much a matter of creative designs as of the skillful adaptation of means to ends. It is craftsmanship of the very highest quality.

He had a sensitive nature. His school days were not happy — public declamations gave him real pain; and when, after the shock of his father's death in 1877, financial stringency made it impossible for him to continue on to college, he was rather glad than otherwise. He was not a good "mixer," and a natural restraint which could easily be mistaken for snobbishness often discouraged friendly-minded people; it also kept fools at a safe distance. But with those whom he had tried and found not wanting he was a charming and delightful conversationalist. An acquaintance once sat with him for an hour on a bench in the Morgan Library while he discoursed freely on an exhibition of modern printing on the walls. Would that that conversation had been recorded!

With his instinct for scholarship, his knowledge of literature, his love of gossip (especially of Bostonians), he would seem naturally to have been directed into the business of publishing, especially as his first work after a short period in the Providence Athenaeum was as a clerk in the house of Houghton, Mifflin & Co. He was under compulsion to earn a living, and this berth was offered through the interest of a relative. But he appears to have had no aptitude for publishing which might have been expected of one of his background and literary tastes. If you take his word for it, he had no aptitude for *anything*. He could not sharpen a pencil, and he knew no more of machinery than a chance visitor to his Press. He tells here and there of his "hatreds," printing included. But that this is a disingenuous generalization can, I think, be proved by his own illuminating statement: In the publishing house it was his duty to clip the notices of the firm's publications which appeared in the various newspapers and journals which came in. He says that he got to know the typographic style and the type of the different papers so that he could tell immediately the source of any clipping.

This aptitude, which must have been a natural one, due to a sensitive eye and mind, goes far indeed to explain why he became a printer. He may have "hated" printing, but the stars in their courses had obviously pre-ordained him for that occupation. His knowledge of type grew with the years, taking final flower in the two-volume *Printing Types, Their History, Forms and Use*. A few more such men who "hate" printing could add a good deal of luster to a profession where, apparently, too many men "just love" it!

Updike was not a sentimentalist. He was too precise, too orderly, and of too cultivated a mind to indulge in the fuzzy marginalia of printing. He was deeply interested in the culture of Europe, and paid many visits there, one or two of long duration. He was never much interested in England (even if he did make continued and early use of English type-faces such as Caslon and Scotch) but found solace in Italy, France, and Spain. There is a somewhat curious anomaly here, and anomalies are not rare in Updike's life. Out of Italy he picked Bodoni as an interest rather than the Venetians; in Spain the hard, sharp clarity of sun and rocks seems to have been more to his mind than the passion of a southern race. For passion seems to have been a quality lacking in his nature as it was in his printing.

In place of such a quality there existed for him the life-long devotion to and love of the Episcopal Church. If in this religious element his nature sublimated any expression of passion, it did so in the direction of order and loyalty. He was a lover of order and decorum in his personal conduct as well as in his printing. In his office, in his town house on Marlboro Street, in his summer house at West Dover in Vermont, order was his as Heaven's first law. A friend tells of calling at the Merrymount Press, and while talking with an employee Updike came into the room for a moment, moved a chair a few inches and made a curt comment on the laxness which had permitted the chair to be out of place.

Nothing was ever out of place in his printing. This is especially to be noted in his work for the church. Of the liturgical requirements of church printing, concerning which he wrote learnedly in an article for *The Dolphin*, he probably knew more than any American printer. Where most printers stumble along, he walked surely. Along with knowledge went faith, which gave his life its direction and afforded what serenity and spiritual peace he was able to attain. Impelled by God and conscience he strove constantly throughout his life to improve his character and his work.

> *Forethought and recollection*
> *Rivet mine armor gay,*
> *The passion of perfection*
> *Redeem my faulty way.*

This quest for perfection kept him humble about his printing, not easily satisfied, and able to take in good part any honest criticism. At the time of the extensive exhibition of his work at the Art Center in 1928, I wrote an appreciation of it for the *Saturday Review of Literature*, and made a short comment on what seemed to me "a semblance of uncertainty and timidity," in the title-pages. In a long and friendly letter written after the review appeared he said:

"As to title-pages, I see what you mean, and it is a very curious thing that if I start a title-page in a bold style, I usually work at it until it is completely toned down. Whether or not I like it that way always is another affair, but that is the way the title-page seems to *want* to be, and I have to let it have its own way. It is odd, isn't it, that problems of this sort seem to have a life of their own, and that in spite of our efforts to turn to the right, they persist in taking the left-hand road?"

IN examining the career of Daniel Berkeley Updike and the Merrymount Press nothing seems so extraordinary as the name he chose for his venture. Why should a quiet, restrained Rhode Islander, a member of the Episcopal Church, after a dozen years of conventional work in a Boston publishing-house and a Cambridge printing-office, setting up for himself after careful thought and planning, and imbued with the cultivation of Europe, confessing an ineptitude for all kinds of physical work, adopt for his new business the long-discredited name of Satan's kingdom of "Merrymount"? What possible affinity could there be between the Thomas Morton "of Cliffords Inne gent," and the Berkeley Updike of Providence? Or between the ragged pine tree on Mount Wollaston and the *fin-de-siècle* printing establishment on Beacon Hill?

Morton was an unregenerate rascal whose one affinity with Updike was his persistence: he pestered the New Canaan for years, returning to these shores as often as he was shipped back to England. Dangerous and forbidden trade with the Indians, exchanging guns and strong drink for pelts, rough and wanton carousing with the natives, a constant feud with the saints of the Bay: these were Morton's activities. Updike was a sober New Englander, though not a Puritan, driven hard by his conscience throughout life, a civilized, almost one may say a super-civilized, man of the nineteenth century, delighting in the indoor sports of conversation and dining-out. His town house on Marlboro Street in Boston was a neat and suitably-appointed residence, his country house on a Vermont hillside as immaculate as even a Vermonter could wish. His talk was precise and almost academic, and he scared off more people by his crisp use of language, his abundant references to anecdotes of the Boston society of his time and the *haute monde* of the eighteenth century, than was good either for them or himself.

In the words of Updike himself, "the Press took its name from the fancy that one could work hard and have a good time," though by his own admission, certainly at the beginning, he got very little fun out of his work. There was a great deal of painful effort and much painful experience in Berkeley Updike's life, and very little play. That he perhaps unconsciously yearned for just what the romantic name of his Press implied may be indicated in this story of a chance encounter between the two men who have made famous the name of Merrymount:

AT .5 Leavitt Street Master William brought together Thomas Morton of Ma-re-mount and Daniel Berkeley Updike of the Merrymount Press. Morton was dressed in the small clothes of his day, Updike in the neat suit of a New England gentleman pursuing a respectable profession. From Morton's belt hung a beaver skin or two, his face was weathered and lined from exposure and long acquaintance with brandy, in sharp contrast to Updike's ascetic countenance.

"Hail, fellow," said Morton, "whence dost thou come?"

An almost imperceptible repugnance showed on Updike's face, yet with courtesy he answered, "I have come from Boston for a friendly visit with our host. And may I ask who thus addresses me — and possibly why?"

"Oh, by the rood, I am known as Tom Morton of Ma-re-mount in the Massachusetts Bay. I have been pestered and tormented by those sectarians of the Old Colony as well as by that canting knave Endicott of Naumkeag, and all, forsooth, because I did set up a may-pole at Ma-re-mount, and bid thither the consorts of my house as well as the Indian lasses in their beaver coats, and there we did celebrate the coming of the spring time in this harsh land. And now, since I have answered you truly and verily as to your inquiry, it behooves you to say with straightforwardness who you are."

Updike of Merrymount answered at once: "I am Daniel Berkeley Updike, a Rhode Islander, and I owned and conducted a business enterprise in Boston where I did printing for those who desired something a little better than ordinary, and I called my shop the Merrymount Press after your gay enterprise at Mount Wollaston. There we printed many things, from little book-labels to large books such as the Book of Common Prayer."

A faint smile added another crease to Morton's face: "The Book of Common Prayer! Such things could not be in my time, for although the neighboring planters of Wessagusset and Shawmut did indeed regard that book as Holy Writ, and even I myself did not fail to claim some acquaintance with it when such did seem to avail me, I marvel that the children of this New Canaan would give leave to have such a book printed within the confines of their patent. If it be not an affront to you, good sir, it cometh to my mind to enquire if you did ever print at your press that admirable book by Dr. Francis Rabelais, or perchance those lively stories of the Italian bastard, Boccaccio, called Il Decamerone, the which was but recently translated into our English tongue. These books we did esteem in our paradise of Ma-re-mount when we were kept within-doors by the great snows, and the keg of Usequebaugh was broached."

"No," answered Updike, "I was never asked to do so by a customer, and I scarcely think I should have been entertained by so doing." His manner piqued Tom Morton.

"And why should any man feel thus about the marvelous doings of Gargantua and Pantagruel, of the lively whimsies of Signor Boccaccio? Did you not see that here were companions worth a man's while when he is alone with no good fellow to join him in a cup of brandy, nor any wenches about with their pretty ways? You surprise me, Updike of Merry-mount. Did you never royster at the tavern, as I have done aforetime with Ben? Have you never pursued the red deer with a musket? Have you never searched the waters of the Narragansetts with line and hook? Have you never danced about the may-pole in the lilac time? Have you never played at bowls? or with battledore and shuttle-cock? Did you in your young days give your time to the reading of the Prayer Book?"

"Mr. Morton, I do not see why we should waste time together. I perhaps owe you a certain debt for the name which we both have used, each to a quite different purpose. And yet your questions disturb me somewhat. In fact they move me, a good deal against my will, to answer you as frankly as you have questioned me. We shall never meet again, nor do I wish to do so. I shall, therefore, speak plainly with you.

"In short, Mr. Morton, I never did any of the things which you ask me about. I had no great abundance of vitality as a boy or later, and I was born with a natural reticence. My ancestors were sober and conscientious men, men of the Roger Williams stamp, not the roysters of Merrymount or of Acomenticus. Not that they were sectarians like the men of Plymouth and Boston and Salem; but they were serious and discreet men. My youth was an earnest time. I had my living to make, and a mother dependent upon me. I thought that I had no time for even the mildest revelry. I am not now so sure that I was either wise or right. In my later years I had two awakenings: once in a time of physical illness, again in a time of great distress of mind. I learned then — as I look backward I realize that I was always learning: it was of the essence of my serious-mindedness — something of life I had never known before. I realized that I had missed something in life — perhaps the clandestine bottle of beer when a boy, perhaps marriage and children, perhaps even that *bon camaraderie* which draws men together in silly little societies. Somehow those two ill-nesses made me realize that however much I accomplished at the trade I had pursued, I had been denied some experiences. *Si jeunesse savait, si vieillesse pouvait!* If the truth must out, I sometimes suspect that it was an unconscious act of self-revelation which made me take the name of your hillock for my press." Updike made almost a gesture of warmth as he put out his hand. "Thomas Morton of Ma-re-mount, hail and farewell. You have done your work and I mine, and we go our ways. Your fight with Endicott and the Puritans is over; my struggle with myself is ended. Will you not believe with me that it is not agreement which we need of each other, but understanding?"

AN EDITOR'S SUMMARY

THE TEXT of this book is a collection of papers written by friends and colleagues about one of the few great printers of the first half of this century. Two of the papers about him were written during Updike's lifetime; four were written shortly after his death in 1941; two were written specially for the present book. The long preliminary essay is the printer's own story of his career.

The book comes naturally therefore to have the defects and virtues of a compilation of this kind. There are, for example, duplications of fact and anecdote, even after numerous editorial surgeries. There is also an occasional and natural tendency in the printer's friends to romanticize him or his attitudes. There is a hesitation to make adverse criticism. These are qualifications which the student would do well to note. On the other hand, the book has the virtue of being an unusal record of opinion, appreciation, and personal experience written down by contemporary specialists who knew intimately the man and his work.

As a man Updike was a curious, a provoking, and a fascinating creature. He was the matured but delicate end-product of a vigorous line of religious colonists. He was excessively shy from boyhood: this shyness was caused or aggravated by physical frailty, by a morbid sensitiveness about his personal appearance (his protruding ears were later improved by plastic surgery), by an intense devotion to a strong-charactered mother, and by the shock of his father's sudden death. As a result of his shyness, Updike was never at ease with life, and could cope with it only by recourse to religion, or by imposing his consciously superior taste and training on those few parts of it — like printing — with which he chose to deal. His sharp wit, his society gossiping with socialite ladies, his pre-occupation with the niceties of living and the exact relationships of society and history, were the effects — or the solutions — of his personal problem.

These personal characteristics helped determine his attitude toward printing and his printing style, and to speak of them is therefore relevant to the purpose of this book. It is obvious that with such a nature as his, Updike could never be a vigorous or creative printer, or a printer devoted to efficiency of production and large volume. But it is equally obvious that he did have the nature to be a most sensitive, tasteful, and scholarly printer, aiming toward exactness of text and arrangement; quick to use the appropriate delicate touch; much concerned with the right effect, but never with the mechanical necessities behind it. (For this last reason Updike was wise and fortunate in selecting John Bianchi as his associate and partner, for Mr. Bianchi, in addition to other qualities, has those of the practical printer, and has been responsible for the mechanization of printing and type-setting at the Merrymount Press.)

The style of Updike's printing was determined not only by his character, but by the times in which he lived. In 1893, when he announced the opening of his Press, our handicraft fashions still were largely English; and long before that date the English industrial revolution had caused life to grow ugly and empty. To fill the physical and spiritual vacuum, a social, artistic, and mechanical medievalism was preached by William Morris; while the "aesthetic" movement, personified in the public mind by Oscar Wilde, made a religion of beauty as an end in itself, finding it in unexpected places, and creating it in unexpected ways.

Both the medieval and the aesthetic cults found expression in printing. No one connected with publishing could have been unaware of the "aesthetic" books published under the Bodley Head imprint, or of Morris' Kelmscott Press books. And both the Bodley Head and Kelmscott books, despite the divergent philosophies behind them, had this much in common: they avoided bareness and they sought to make decoration integral. (Some Victorian books were anything but bare; but their publishers, like housewives of the time, used chromos and knick-knacks to conceal the vacuum.)

In his very first announcement, Updike showed he was

responsive to what was going on in England. He besought the patronage of those who desired "decorative printing"; he announced he would keep informed of the "best English, French and American work that he may be enabled to give books those touches which are nowadays necessary"; he spoke of "initials and bordered title-pages in the modern aesthetic English style."

As we go down the years of a collection of Merrymount books we see first some of the early books made with this manifesto in mind, made often with the co-operation of leading English artists. We then see the budding typographical scholar, aroused by Morris' revivalisms, trying his hand at books with a Colonial flavor, a Venetian flavor, an English 1795 flavor. This allusive trick he gradually abandoned (except for special books which called for it) in favor of a simple honest style which harmonized with his own instinct for neatness and propriety, and which — as Mr. Rollins remarks in his essay — he had seen around him in his own days of apprenticeship.

This style often suggests English printing of about 1800. Most of the types Updike had collected were suited to such a style, and its virtues of clarity, regularity, and dignity were entirely suited to his nature. It had the further virtue of being practically fool-proof — important in a growing plant where more and more work passed across his desk on its way to the composing-room and press-room.

The other characteristics of Merrymount books are easily described. Their papers have varied from imported hand-made to good simple domestic. As the years went on, the tendency has been more and more to use paper of good substance but free of any irregularity in its color or its finish. The press-work almost always has been excellent, the customary short runs and smooth papers helping to achieve this excellence. Color, mostly red and brown, has been used moderately, and generally only on title-pages. Decoration usually has consisted of simple head-bands of printers' flowers (often Updike's own European discoveries) and reproductions of old engraved head-pieces. At one period a number of decorations were specially drawn by Cleland and Dwiggins, usually in historical styles. The bindings have been various: cloth or paper sides stamped with drawn decorations; patterned paper sides with simple gold-stamped cloth spines; and all linen, usually black, with simple gold stamping on the spines only.

The books Updike printed were for New York and other trade publishers, for book clubs, for booksellers, for private individuals, for businesses, and for himself as his own publisher. He became a sort of specialist in privately-printed memoirs, diaries, memorials, and books of verse. He was also a specialist in liturgical printing. In only a very few cases was he the printer of already-famous books — a field in which it would have been instructive to compare his editions with those of other great printers of the past.

Individually the smaller Merrymount books may sometimes give the impression of being too simple to be "fine" printing, and we may therefore tend to look to the few larger books as more monumental evidence of Updike's greatness as a printer. But the assembled hundreds of smaller Merrymount books — all of them well-planned, well-printed, tastefully designed, scrupulously edited and proof-read — is irrefutable and overwhelming evidence of Updike's assured high place in the annals of the craft.

Thanks are due to the authors and original publishers of essays in this book for their gracious permissions to reprint them here. Special thanks are due to George Parker Winship, Rudolph Ruzicka and Lawrence C. Wroth for special help.

PETER BEILENSON

A GALLERY OF
MERRYMOUNT TITLE-PAGES
AND
MERRYMOUNT TYPES

THE following gallery of Merrymount title-pages is an attempt to show the variety of styles used at the Press from its beginnings until Updike's death. These pages are not arranged in chronological order, but are grouped (so far as possible) by styles. Since Updike was occasionally away from his desk for long periods, a few of the pages shown are apt to be Mr. Bianchi's work in whole or part.

Merrymount text-pages are not shown in this collection because they generally depend for their effects on good type, well-arranged on the page, and well-printed on good paper. Such virtues must be seen in the actual books to be appreciated. The inclusion of such pages here in line-cuts would not do them justice; nor could they compare in interest with the title-pages. Incidental printing from the Press, also not shown here, may be studied in reproduction in the two books about Updike written by George Parker Winship, published respectively by Herbert Reichner, Vienna, 1929, and by The Printing House of Leo Hart, Rochester, 1947.

The editor wishes to thank Mr. Bianchi for permitting him to choose these examples from all of the hundreds of Merrymount books on the library shelves of the Press itself, and for supplying the specimen pages of Merrymount types which follow the title-pages.

ELIGION IN
LITERATURE
AND RELIGION
IN LIFE. BEING
TWO PAPERS
WRITTEN BY
STOPFORD A.
BROOKE, M.A.,
LL.D.

THOMAS Y. CROWELL & COMPANY
NEW YORK. ANNO DOMINI MDCCCCI

WHAT·IS·WORTH·WHILE?
BY·ANNA·ROBERTSON·BROWN

THOMAS·Y·CROWELL·&·COMPANY
NEW·YORK·&·BOSTON

THE UNFOLDING LIFE

PASSAGES FROM THE DIARIES, NOTE-BOOKS AND LETTERS OF HOWARD MUNRO LONGYEAR, AND FROM THE LETTERS HE RECEIVED FROM HIS PARENTS AND FRIENDS. ARRANGED AND EDITED BY HENRY D. NUNN

PRIVATELY PRINTED AT THE MERRY-MOUNT PRESS, BOSTON, A.D. MDCCCCI

THE HISTORY

OF THE

CLASS OF 'SIXTY-NINE

AMHERST COLLEGE

1889–1894

"Light"

PRINTED FOR THE CLASS

1894

THE
PAROCHIAL
LIBRARY
of the
𝔈𝔦𝔤𝔥𝔱𝔢𝔢𝔫𝔱𝔥 𝔆𝔢𝔫𝔱𝔲𝔯𝔶
in
CHRIST CHURCH
BOSTON

By
A *Proprietor* of CHRIST CHURCH

BOSTON
Privately printed at the *Merrymount Press* in the
Year of our LORD MDCCCCXVII

THE
PREFACE
TO
Johnson's
DICTIONARY
OF THE
English Language
1755

CLEVELAND
THE ROWFANT CLUB
1934

Great Riches

By Charles W. Eliot, LL.D.

President of Harvard University

New York

Thomas Y. Crowell & Co.

Publishers

The Old Year
And the New

BY

CHARLES EDWARD JEFFERSON

PASTOR OF BROADWAY TABERNACLE
NEW YORK

New York
THOMAS Y. CROWELL & CO.
PUBLISHERS

THE DEFENCE OF POESIE
A LETTER TO Q. ELIZABETH
A DEFENCE OF LEICESTER
BY SIR PHILIP SIDNEY

EDITED BY G. E. WOODBERRY

THE MERRYMOUNT PRESS
BOSTON : MDCCCCVIII

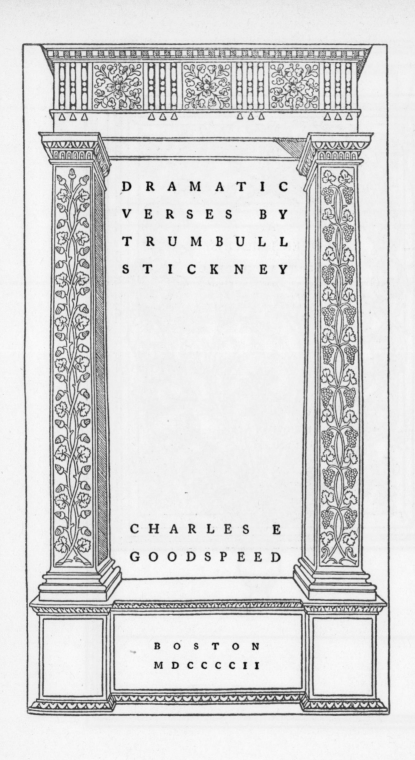

DRAMATIC
VERSES BY
TRUMBULL
STICKNEY

CHARLES E
GOODSPEED

BOSTON
MDCCCCII

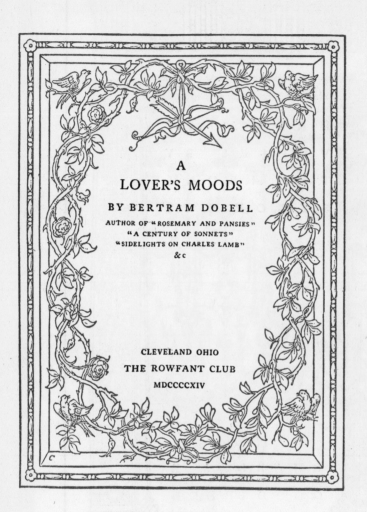

A
LOVER'S MOODS

BY BERTRAM DOBELL
AUTHOR OF "ROSEMARY AND PANSIES"
"A CENTURY OF SONNETS"
"SIDELIGHTS ON CHARLES LAMB"
& c

CLEVELAND OHIO
THE ROWFANT CLUB
MDCCCCXIV

THE GREATER INCLINATION
BY EDITH WHARTON

CHARLES SCRIBNER'S
SONS, NEW YORK: 1899

CHRISTOPHER
IN HIS
SPORTING JACKET

BY

John Wilson

[CHRISTOPHER NORTH]

Illustrated

New York

McCLURE, PHILLIPS & CO.

1901

THE SUCCESS OF DEFEAT

BY

Maltbie D. Babcock, D.D.

NEW YORK
Charles Scribner's Sons
1905

Bread and Honey

BY

FRANCES H. SAVAGE

NEW YORK

PRIVATELY PRINTED

1939

HARVEST–TIDE

A BOOK OF VERSES

BY SIR LEWIS MORRIS, Knt., M.A.

NEW YORK
T. Y. CROWELL & COMPANY
1901

THE PERSONALITY OF
THOREAU

BY F. B. SANBORN

BOSTON
CHARLES E. GOODSPEED
1901

LETTERS
FROM ROWLAND HAZARD
TO HIS WIFE
WRITTEN IN THE YEAR
1876

PRIVATELY PRINTED

1916

A CATALOGUE

OF THE ENGRAVED PLATES
FOR
PICTURESQUE VIEWS
IN ENGLAND AND WALES
WITH
NOTES AND COMMENTARIES
. .

COMPILED BY
FRANCIS BULLARD

BOSTON
PRIVATELY PRINTED
MDCCCCX

A CHOICE OF BOOKS
FROM
THE LIBRARY OF
ISABELLA STEWART GARDNER
FENWAY COURT

MDCCCCVI

THE GOLDEN OPPORTUNITY
An Address

DELIVERED AT THE FOURTH ANNUAL CON-
VENTION OF THE AMERICAN NATIONAL
RETAIL JEWELERS ASSOCIATION OMAHA
NEBRASKA WEDNESDAY AUGUST 4 1909 BY

ERNEST MILLER LUNT

PRINTED FOR THE
TOWLE MANUFACTURING COMPANY
NEWBURYPORT MASSACHUSETTS
AT THE MERRYMOUNT PRESS
BOSTON

THOREAU
THE POET-NATURALIST

WITH MEMORIAL VERSES

BY WILLIAM ELLERY CHANNING

NEW EDITION, ENLARGED
EDITED BY F. B. SANBORN

MY GREATEST SKILL HAS BEEN TO WANT BUT LITTLE. FOR
JOY I COULD EMBRACE THE EARTH. I SHALL DELIGHT TO BE
BURIED IN IT. AND THEN I THINK OF THOSE AMONG MEN, WHO
WILL KNOW THAT I LOVE THEM, THOUGH I TELL THEM NOT.
H. D. T.

CHARLES E. GOODSPEED
BOSTON: 1902

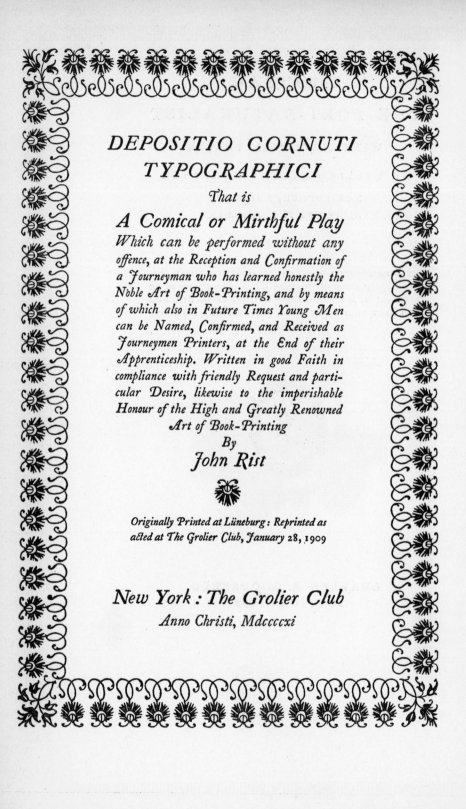

DEPOSITIO CORNUTI TYPOGRAPHICI

That is

A Comical or Mirthful Play

Which can be performed without any
offence, at the Reception and Confirmation of
a Journeyman who has learned honestly the
Noble Art of Book-Printing, and by means
of which also in Future Times Young Men
can be Named, Confirmed, and Received as
Journeymen Printers, at the End of their
Apprenticeship. Written in good Faith in
compliance with friendly Request and particular Desire, likewise to the imperishable
Honour of the High and Greatly Renowned
Art of Book-Printing

By

John Rist

*Originally Printed at Lüneburg: Reprinted as
acted at The Grolier Club, January 28, 1909*

New York: The Grolier Club

Anno Christi, Mdccccxi

A
NOTABLE LIBEL CASE

The Criminal Prosecution of
Theodore Lyman Jr. by Daniel Webster
in the
Supreme Judicial Court of Massachusetts
November Term 1828

——

JOSIAH H. BENTON Jr.

BOSTON
Charles E. Goodspeed
1904

Forty
Modern Fables
By
George Ade

New York
R. H. Russell
1901

WAR BOOKS

By
H. M. TOMLINSON

A Lecture
Given at Manchester University
February 15, 1929

THE ROWFANT CLUB
Cleveland, Ohio
1930

POEMS

OF

TENNYSON

CHOSEN AND EDITED WITH

AN INTRODUCTION

BY

HENRY VAN DYKE

BOSTON, U. S. A.

GINN & COMPANY, PUBLISHERS

1903

The
Complete Angler
OR
THE CONTEMPLATIVE MAN'S
RECREATION
BY IZAAK WALTON

WITH AN INTRODUCTION BY
BLISS PERRY
AND DECORATIONS BY
W. A. DWIGGINS

Boston
C. E. GOODSPEED & CO.
1928

THE VOYAGE OF THE
OREGON
FROM SAN FRANCISCO
TO SANTIAGO IN
1898
AS TOLD BY
ONE OF THE CREW

PRIVATELY PRINTED
THE MERRYMOUNT PRESS
BOSTON
1908

SANCTUARY

BY

EDITH WHARTON

WITH ILLUSTRATIONS BY
WALTER APPLETON CLARK

CHARLES SCRIBNER'S SONS
NEW YORK : MDCCCCIII

PRINTING TYPES

THEIR HISTORY, FORMS, AND USE

A STUDY IN SURVIVALS

BY

DANIEL BERKELEY UPDIKE

WITH ILLUSTRATIONS

*"Nunca han tenido, ni tienen las artes otros
enemigos que los ignorantes"*

VOLUME I

CAMBRIDGE

HARVARD UNIVERSITY PRESS

LONDON: HUMPHREY MILFORD

OXFORD UNIVERSITY PRESS

1922

OLD AGE & IMMORTALITY
AN ADDRESS
DELIVERED BEFORE THE WORCESTER
FIRE SOCIETY AT ITS CENTENNIAL
JANUARY 21, 1893
BY
GEORGE FRISBIE HOAR

WORCESTER
1904

John Shaw Billings

CREATOR OF THE NATIONAL MEDICAL LIBRARY
AND ITS CATALOGUE
FIRST DIRECTOR OF THE NEW YORK
PUBLIC LIBRARY

BY

HARRY MILLER LYDENBERG

CHIEF REFERENCE LIBRARIAN OF THE
NEW YORK PUBLIC LIBRARY

Chicago
AMERICAN LIBRARY ASSOCIATION
1924

SIDNEY LAWTON SMITH

DESIGNER, ETCHER, ENGRAVER

With Extracts from his Diary
and a Check-list of his
Bookplates

BOSTON
Charles E. Goodspeed & Co.
1931

THE EDUCATION OF HENRY ADAMS

AN AUTOBIOGRAPHY

◆ ◆ ◆

ILLUSTRATED WITH TWELVE ETCHINGS BY

SAMUEL CHAMBERLAIN

AND WITH AN INTRODUCTION BY

HENRY SEIDEL CANBY

BOSTON: PRINTED FOR THE MEMBERS OF

THE LIMITED EDITIONS CLUB

AT THE MERRYMOUNT PRESS

1942

Specimen

LETTRE BATARDE   *Acquired 1901*

The name of The Merrymount Press is derived from
the ancient estate of a certain Thomas Morton, a very
sturdy Englishman, who with a company of friends
emigrated to New England in 1628. Bradford, in the
second book of his History of Plymouth, says: "Aboute
some three or four years before this time, there came
over one Captaine Wollastone (a man of pretie parts),
& with him three or four more of some eminencie, who

LETTRE DE SOMME   *Acquired 1901*

brought with them a great many servants, with provisions & other impla//
ments for to begine a plantation; and pitched themselves in a place within
the Massachusets, which they called, after their Captaine's name, Mount//
Wollaston. Amongst whom was one Mr. Morton, who, it should seem, had
some small adventure (of his owne or other mens) amongst them." Morton,
with the others, settled at Wollaston, near Quincy, calling his house Ma//re
Mount, or Merrymount; a name still attaching to that locality. About the
character of Morton, opinions differ. By some he is described as a roystering,
worthless fellow, who made Merrymount the scene of carousal and the home
of the idle ne'er//do//well. Others have painted his picture as that of an easy//

PICA ENGLISH BLACK   *Acquired 1898*

going country gentleman, more Cavalier than
Roundhead in his tendencies, whose attachment
to the Church of England led to malignment by
his Puritan neighbours. Probably neither one
nor yet the other view is true. But it is true that
he made Merrymount the scene of old English
sports, and that he there set up a Maypole; per=
haps as a protest against the gloomy life of the

The Merrymount Press

Puritans. Morton, in that odd old book, The New English Canaan, says that "the Inhabitants of Pason-agessit, (having translated the name of their habitation from that ancient Salvage name to Ma-re Mount, and being resolved to have the new name confirmed for a memorial to after ages,) did devise amongst themselves to have it performed in a solemne manner, with Revels and merriment after the old English custome; [they] prepared to sett up a

Maypole upon the festivall day of Philip and Jacob, and therefore brewed a barrell of excellent beare and provided a case of bottles, to be spent, with other good cheare, for all comers of that day. And because they would have it in a compleat forme, they had prepared a song fitting to the time and present occasion. And upon Mayday they brought the Maypole to the place appointed, with drumes, gunnes, pistols and other fitting instruments, for that purpose; and there erected it with

the help of Salvages, that came thither of purpose to see the manner of our Revels. A goodly pine tree of 80. foote longe was reared up, with a peare of buckshorns nayled one somewhat neare unto the top of it: where it stood, as a faire sea marke for directions how to finde out the way to mine Host of Ma-re Mount." As to the real Morton, the reader may suit his own prejudices, which, if adverse,

Specimen of Types

Janson Italic

may be made more so by the biographical sketch prefixed to an edition of Morton's New English Canaan; or if more favourable, by Hawthorne's pretty web of romance spun around The Maypole of Merrymount in Twice-Told Tales. It is enough for the purpose of The Merrymount Press, if, in disregard of any analogies or paradoxes with which curious persons bewilder themselves, we regard the Maypole as a symbol of happiness found in workaday things; of a high aim and pleasure in trying to attain it,

Caslon Italic

an ideal to which The Merrymount Press has always endeavoured to be true. The name of The Merrymount Press is derived from the ancient estate of a certain Thomas Morton, which now gives title to a suburb of Quincy. He was a sturdy Englishman, who with a company of friends emigrated to New England in 1628. Bradford, in the second book of his History of Plymouth, says: "Aboute some three or four years before this time, there came over one Captaine Wollastone (a man of pretie parts), & with him three or four more of some eminen-

Mountjoye (Bell) Italic

cie, who brought with them a great many servants, with provisions & other implaments for to begine a plantation; and pitched themselves in a place within the Massachusets, which they called, after their Captaine's name, Mount-Wollaston. Amongst whom was one Mr. Morton, who, it should seem, had some small adventure (of his owne or other mens) amongst them." Morton, with the others, settled at Wollaston,

The Merrymount Press

near Quincy, calling his house Ma-re Mount, or Merrymount; a name still attaching to that locality. About the
character of Morton, opinions differ. By some he is described as a roystering, worthless fellow, who made Merrymount the scene of carousal and the home of the idle
ne'er-do-well. Others have painted his picture as that of an
easy-going country gentleman, more Cavalier than Roundhead in his tendencies, whose attachment to the Church
of England led to malignment by his Puritan neighbours.

Probably neither one nor yet the other view is true.
But it is true that he made Merrymount a scene of old
English sports, and that he there set up a Maypole;
perhaps as a protest against the gloomy life of the Puritans. Morton, in that odd old book, The New English Canaan, says that "the Inhabitants of Pasonages-
sit, (having translated the name of their habitation
from that ancient Salvage name to Ma-re Mount, and
being resolved to have the new name confirmed for a

memorial to after ages,) did devise amongst themselves to have it performed in a solemne manner,
with Revels and merriment after the old English
custome; [they] prepared to sett up a Maypole
upon the festivall day of Philip and Jacob, and
therefore brewed a barrell of excellent beare and
provided a case of bottles, to be spent, with other
good cheare, for all comers of that day. And because they would have it in a compleat forme,

Specimen of Types

Oxford Italic

they had prepared a song fitting to the time and present occasion. And upon Mayday they brought the Maypole to the place appointed, with drumes, gunnes, pistols and other fitting instruments, for that purpose; and there erected it with the help of Salvages, that came thither of purpose to see the manner of our Revels. A goodly pine tree of 80. foote longe was reared up, with a peare of buckshorns nayled one somewhat neare unto the top of it: where it stood, as a faire sea marke for directions how to find out the way to mine Host

Scotch–face Italic

of Ma-re Mount." As to the real Morton, the reader may suit his own prejudices, which, if adverse, may be made more so by the biographical sketch prefixed to an edition of Morton's New English Canaan; or if more favourable, by Hawthorne's pretty web of romance spun around The Maypole of Merrymount in Twice-Told Tales. It is enough for the purpose of The Merrymount Press, if, in disregard of any analogies or paradoxes with which curious persons bewilder themselves,

French Script   *Acquired 1910*

we regard the Maypole as a symbol of happiness found in workaday things; of a high aim and pleasure in trying to attain it, an ideal to which The Merrymount Press has always endeavoured to be true.

The name of The Merrymount Press is derived from the ancient estate of a certain Thomas Morton, which now gives title to a suburb of Quincy. He was a sturdy Englishman, who with a company of friends

The Merrymount Press

BODONI *Acquired 1930*

emigrated to New England in 1628. Bradford, in
the second book of his History of Plymouth, says:
"Aboute some three or four years before this time,
there came over one Captaine Wollastone (a man
of pretie parts), & with him three or four more of
some eminencie, who brought with them a great
many servants, with provisions & other implaments for to begine a plantation; and pitched themselves in a place within the Massachusets, which

POLIPHILUS *Acquired 1925*

they called, after their Captaine's name, Mount-Wollaston. Amongst whom was one Mr. Morton, who, it should
seem, had some small adventure (of his owne or other
mens) amongst them." Morton, with the others, settled at
Wollaston, near Quincy, calling his house Ma-re Mount,
or Merrymount; a name still attaching to that locality.
About the character of Morton, opinions differ. By some
he is described as a roystering, worthless fellow, who
made Merrymount the scene of carousal and the home of

LUTETIA *Acquired 1927*

the idle ne'er-do-well. Others have painted his picture as
that of an easy-going country gentleman, more Cavalier
than Roundhead in his tendencies, whose attachment to
the Church of England led to malignment by his Puritan
neighbours. Probably neither one nor yet the other view
is true. But it is true that he made Merrymount the scene
of old English sports, and that he there set up a Maypole;
perhaps as a protest against the gloomy life of the Puritans. Morton, in that odd old book, The New English

Specimen of Types

BODONI ITALIC

Canaan, says that "the Inhabitants of Pasonages-sit, (having translated the name of their habitation from that ancient Salvage name to Ma-re Mount, and being resolved to have the new name confirmed for a memorial to after ages,) did devise amongst themselves to have it performed in a solemne manner, with Revels and merriment after the old English custome; [they] prepared to sett up a Maypole upon the festivall day of Philip and Jacob, and

BLADO

therefore brewed a barrell of excellent beare and provided a case of bottles, to be spent, with other good cheare, for all comers of that day. And because they would have it in a compleat forme, they had prepared a song fitting to the time and present occasion. And upon Mayday they brought the Maypole to the place appointed, with drumes, gunnes, pistols and other fitting instruments, for that purpose; and there erected it with the help of Salvages, that came thither of purpose to see the manner of our Revels. A goodly pine tree of 80. foote longe was reared up, with a peare

LUTETIA ITALIC

of buckshorns nayled one somewhat neare unto the top of it: where it stood, as a faire sea marke for directions how to finde out the way to mine Host of Ma-re Mount." As to the real Morton, the reader may suit his own prejudices, which, if adverse, may be made more so by the biographical sketch prefixed to an edition of Morton's New English Canaan; or if more favourable, by Hawthorne's pretty web of romance spun around The Maypole of Merrymount in Twice-Told Tales. It is enough for the purpose of The Merrymount Press, if in disregard of any analogies or paradoxes with which

The Merrymount Press

MONTALLEGRO (NO ITALIC)   *Acquired 1904*
curious persons bewilder themselves, we regard
the Maypole as a symbol of happiness found in
workaday things; of a high aim and pleasure in
trying to attain it, an ideal to which The Merrymount Press has always endeavoured to be true.

MERRYMOUNT (NO ITALIC)   *Acquired 1894*
The name of the Merrymount Press
is derived from the ancient estate of a
certain Thomas Morton, a sturdy Englishman, who with a company of friends
emigrated to New England in 1628.

The above types were specially cut for the Press
Herbert Horne designing the Montallegro
and Bertram Grosvenor Goodhue
the Merrymount fount

THIS EDITION HAS BEEN PRINTED FOR THE AMERICAN INSTITUTE
OF GRAPHIC ARTS BY PETER BEILENSON, MOUNT VERNON, AND
BOUND BY THE RUSSELL RUTTER COMPANY, NEW YORK